BUTTERFLIES & D.
A Site Guide

PAUL HILL & COLIN TWIST

Line drawings by Dan Powell
Cover illustration by David Koster

ARLEQUIN

ISBN 1 900159 05 8

First published 1996
Second edition 1998

Arlequin Press, 26 Broomfield Road, Chelmsford, Essex CM1 1SW
Telephone: 01245 267771
© Paul Hill & Colin Twist
All maps © Arlequin Press
A catalogue record for this book is available.

CONTENTS

SITE MAP KEY

1. Ainsdale Hills, Merseyside	BD	64. Lydlinch Common, Dorset	B
2. Anderton Nature Park, Cheshire	BD	65. Mabie Forest, Dumphries & Galloway	B
3. Arne RSPB Reserve, Dorset	BD	66. Magdalen Hill Down, Hampshire	B
4. Arnside Knott, Cumbria	B	67. Martin Down NNR, Hampshire	B
5. Ashberry Pasture, Yorkshire	B	68. Mill Lawn Brook, Hampshire	D
6. Aston Rowant, Oxfordshire	B	69. Milton Country Park, Cambridgeshire	D
7. Atcham & Berrington Pool, Shropshire	D	70. Monkwood, Worcestershire	B
8. Aylesbeare Common RSPB Reserve, Devon	BD	71. Nagshead RSPB Reserve, Gloucestershire	BD
9. Ballard Down, Dorset	B	72. Narborough Railway Line, Norfolk	B
10. Barnack Hills & Holes NNR, Northamptonshire	B	73. National Dragonfly Museum, Northamptonshire	D
11. Barton Hills NNR, Bedfordshire	B	74. New Bridge, West Sussex	D
12. Beinn Eighe NNR, Highland	D	75. Noar Hill, Hampshire	B
13. Bentley Station Meadow, Hampshire	B	76. Northward Hill RSPB Reserve, Kent	B
14. Bentley Wood, Wiltshire	B	77. Oaken Wood, Surrey	B
15. Bernwood Forest, Oxfordshire	B	78. Oxwich NNR, Glamorgan	B
16. Big Waters, Northumberland	BD	79. Park Corner Heath, East Sussex	B
17. Black Lake, Cheshire	D	80. Pegsdon Hills, Bedfordshire	B
18. Brampton Wood, Cambridgeshire	B	81. Plymbridge Wood, Devon	B
19. Brandesburton Ponds, Humberside	D	82. Prees Heath, Shropshire	B
20. Braunton Burrows, Devon	BD	83. Prestbury Hill, Gloucestershire	B
21. Bridge of Grudie, Highland	D	84. Prestwood Picnic Site, Buckinghamshire	B
22. Brigton Pond, Dumphries & Galloway	BD	85. Red Moor, Cornwall	BD
23. Broadcroft Quarry, Dorset	B	86. Red Rocks Marsh, Merseyside	B
24. Broughton Down, Hampshire	B	87. Risley Moss & Rixton Claypits, Cheshire	D
25. Brynberian, Dyfed	D	88. Rivacre Valley, Cheshire	BD
26. Castle Eden Dene, County Durham	B	89. River Avon, Lacock Abbey, Wiltshire	D
27. Claife Heights, Cumbria	D	90. River Dee, Cheshire	D
28. Compton Bay, Isle of Wight	B	91. River Waveney & Castle Marshes, Suffolk	D
29. Cornmill Meadows, Essex	D	92. Ryton Wood, Warwickshire	D
30. Cors Bodgynydd, Gwynedd	D	93. St Abbs Head, Borders	B
31. Craigellachie NNR, Highland	B	94. Sewell Cutting, Bedfordshire	B
32. Cunsey Beck, Cumbria	D	95. Silver Flowe, Dumphries & Galloway	BD
33. Dowrog Common, Dyfed	BD	96. Slapton Ley, Devon	D
34. Dunkery Hill, Somerset	B	97. Smardale Gill, Cumbria	B
35. Durlston Country Park, Dorset	B	98. Southrey Wood, Lincolnshire	D
36. East Blean Wood, Kent	B	99. Spean Bridge, Highland	D
37. Esher Common, Surrey	D	100. Stoke Camp, Somerset	B
38. Felmersham Gravel Pits, Bedfordshire	D	101. Strumpshaw Fen RSPB Reserve, Norfolk	BD
39. Feoch Meadows, Strathclyde	BD	102. Studland Heath NNR, Dorset	BD
40. Fleetwith, Cumbria	B	103. Thursley Common, Surrey	D
41. Frost's Common, Norfolk	D	104. Trench Wood, Worcestershire	B
42. Gait Barrows NNR, Lancashire	B	105. Ufton Fields, Warwickshire	B
43. Glapthorn Cow Pasture, Northamptonshire	B	106. Upton Fen, Norfolk	D
44. Glasdrum Wood, Strathclyde	B	107. Vale Royal Locks, Cheshire	D
45. Glen Affric, Highland	D	108. Warnham Nature Reserve, Surrey	D
46. Glen Moss, Strathclyde	D	109. Warton Crag, Lancashire	B
47. Great Orme, Llandudno, Gwynedd	B	110. Watlington Hill, Oxfordshire	B
48. Haldon Woods, Devon	B	111. Welney WWT Reserve, Cambridgeshire	D
49. Hatchet Pond & Crockford Bridge, Hampshire	BD	112. Welsh Moor, Glamorgan	B
50. Hordle Cliff, Hampshire	B	113. Wheldrake Ings NNR, Yorkshire	BD
51. Itchen Valley Country Park, Hampshire	BD	114. Whisby Nature Park, Lincolnshire	BD
52. Johnny Brown's Common Area, Yorkshire	D	115. Whitbarrow Scar, Cumbria	B
53. Kenfig NNR, Glamorgan	D	116. Whitecross Green Wood, Oxfordshire	B
54. Kingsbury Water Park, Warwickshire	D	117. Whixall Moss, Shropshire	BD
55. Kiplingcotes Chalk Pit, Humberside	B	118. Wicken Fen NNR, Cambridgeshire	D
56. Lake Vyrnwy RSPB Reserve, Powys	B	119. Wirral Way, Merseyside & Cheshire	B
57. Lathkill Dale, Derbyshire	B	120. Wolves Wood RSPB Reserve, Suffolk	B
58. Lenwade Water, Norfolk	D	121. Wood of Cree, Dumphries & Galloway	B
59. Little Breach, Devon	B	122. Woodwalton Fen NNR, Huntingdonshire	D
60. Little Scrubs Meadow, Lincolnshire	B	123. Woolsthorpe Line, Lincolnshire	D
61. Llanymynech Quarry, Shropshire	B	124. Wyre Forest, Shropshire, Herefordshire &	
62. Loch Bran, Highland	D	Worcestershire	B
63. Logierait Wood Pool, Tayside	D	125. Ynys-Hir RSPB Reserve, Powys	BD

4

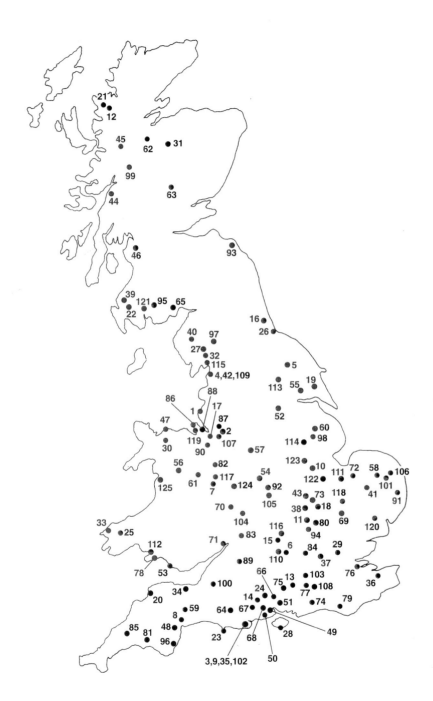

INTRODUCTION

The aim of this book is to enable the reader to see all the breeding butterflies and dragonflies in Great Britain.

The majority of the sites featured have been visited by the authors at the time when the target species are on the wing. This enables us to clearly indicate the prime time to visit in an average year. Timing, combined with exact location and sunshine are the factors which should produce the best results.

Regular visitors to some sites may find species omitted from the lists. This is usually owing to small numbers being present which do not offer a sporting chance of a successful sighting, or the authors have not visited during the flight period.

The choice of the locations used has been determined by the abundance of the target species and by geographical location. Some of the sites, for instance, are in the North of England where there are outlying colonies of species with a mainly southerly distribution. Sites where there is no public access, or for where a permit is required (unless one is readily available), have been omitted, as have sites with a fragile or unsafe terrain.

Many of the sites chosen have some degree of protection, either through designation as Sites of Special Scientific Interest (SSSI's), or Local or National Nature Reserves (LNR's or NNR's). Most are sites well known for their entomological interest. We do not feel that disclosure of any of the sites is advertising them to the few collectors that still operate. In some cases collectors know of more sites than the conservationists!

The Large Blue and Large Copper are reintroductions so do not feature in the main sites section of the book. The same applies to Large Tortoiseshell, which does not (as yet) have any self-sustaining colonies and so is considered to be extinct as a breeding species. Species with a wide distribution and which may be encountered when seeking out target species are not specifically mentioned in the text.

The layout of the book is self-explanatory. The timings given are the optimum periods to visit each site to see the most species in one visit, but some sites require several visits to see all the target species. We hope that the frustration of finding locations for target species and the correct timing of visits will now be avoided. We also hope that the book will encourage readers to seek new sites which may in turn receive some sort of protection. On the maps, arrows indicate optimum viewing areas.

Looking for dragonflies and butterflies is an exercise carried out in fine weather and in usually pleasant surroundings. It also enables enthusiasts to observe other aspects of the natural world including birds and plants. The best opportunities for this are highlighted in the text. We hope this book will provide further stimulus to the experienced and give the inexperienced the opportunity to embark on what we believe is an absorbing pastime.

The production of this book would not have been possible without the help of many individuals who updated us on the status of various species at some of the sites. Nor would it have been possible without the permission of the various organisations who have allowed us to publicise their sites. In particular we would like to thank the following:

Ted Abraham, Peter Beale, Mel Bellingham, Bill Booth, Dick and Jan Brown, Jeff Clarke, Chris Felton, Lee Hall, Edwin Hopkins, George Hunter, John Jones, Dr Ralf Kirkwood, Frank Lockley, Bob Maton, Doug Messenger, Brian Mnew, Julia Mottishaw, Ian Newton, David Paddiley, Bryan Roberts, Barry Shaw, Mike Slater, Don Tagg, Rob Whitehead and Steve Young.

We are particularly indebted to John Stevens for his assistance with southern sites.

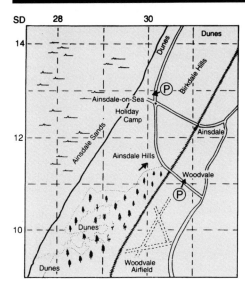

Grid Ref: SD 300 115
O.S. Map: 108

ACCESS
Open access along public footpaths except for Ainsdale NNR, for which a permit is required for access off the paths. Park near the holiday camp at Ainsdale-on-Sea, or at Woodvale.

HABITAT
A range of duneland habitats bordered by woodland, much of which is introduced conifers.

STATUS
National Nature Reserve.

TARGET SPECIES
Dark Green Fritillary (*Argynnis aglaja*); Grayling (*Hipparchia semele*).

TIMING
All July to August week 2 for Dark Green Fritillary and Grayling. Early July probably the best.

OTHER SPECIES
A wide range of common species for the habitat are present. Good numbers of Yellow-wing Darter (*Sympetrum flaveolum*) were recorded in the Birkdale Dunes in August 1995.

OTHER FLORA AND FAUNA
Common Lizard, Sand Lizard and Natterjack Toad. Red Squirrel at Formby (SD 280 083). Pendulous Green Flowered Helleborine and Dune Helleborine in early to mid-July.

OTHER INFORMATION
Contact: Sefton Ranger Service at Formby Council Offices, Freshfield Road, Formby, Merseyside.

English Nature, Ainsdale NNR Office, 2 West End Lodge, Pinfold Lane, Southport, Merseyside.

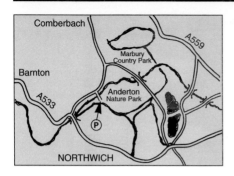

Grid Ref: SJ 649 753 (car park)
O.S. Map: 118

ACCESS
Public access. From the car park follow the paths towards the river.

HABITAT
Small ponds, developing Birch woodland and calcareous grassland.

STATUS
Country Park managed by Cheshire County Council.

TARGET SPECIES
Emperor Dragonfly (*Anax imperator*); Purple Hairstreak (*Quercusia quercus*).

TIMING
Late June and throughout July for Emperor; July week 3 to August week 2 for Purple Hairstreak.

OTHER SPECIES
Nineteen species of dragon and damselfly (12 breeding) and approximately 30 species of butterfly have been recorded in the general area.

OTHER FLORA AND FAUNA
The site is good for most common bird species. The calcareous grasslands contain an interesting range of plants for the area including Creeping Willow and Fragrant Orchid. Nearby Neumann's Flash and Marbury Country Park are good birdwatching venues.

OTHER INFORMATION
A range of leaflets (all free) about the area and its natural history are available. Contact: Cheshire County Council Countryside Management Service, Marbury Country Park, Comberbach, Northwich, Cheshire or Witton Area Conservation Group, c/o 1 Clive Cottage, London Road, Allostock, Knutsford, Cheshire WA16 9LT.

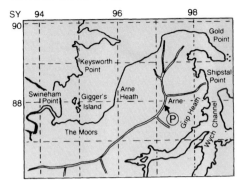

Grid Ref: SY 972 878
O.S. Map: 195

ACCESS
Public access to Shipstal Point and nature trails. Park in RSPB car park.

HABITAT
Dry lowland heath, scattered coniferous and deciduous woodland.

STATUS
RSPB Nature Reserve, SSSI.

TARGET SPECIES
Small Red Damselfly (*Ceriagrion tenellum*); Migrant Hawker (*Aeshna mixta*); Downy Emerald (*Cordulia aenea*); Grayling (*Hipparchia semele*); White Admiral (*Ladoga camilla*); Silver-studded Blue (*Plebejus argus*).

TIMING
July week 3 to August week 4 is suitable for all the target species except Downy Emerald which flies from May week 4 to July week 2.

OTHER SPECIES
Twenty-two species of dragonfly and thirty-three of butterfly have been recorded.

OTHER FLORA AND FAUNA
Dartford Warbler, Hobby and Nightjar. Waders at Shipstal Point can be seen from the hide.

OTHER INFORMATION
Several ponds have been created to benefit dragonflies on the reserve. These are best observed from the path that leads to the hide at Shipstal Point. An interpretative board is situated next to the ponds.

Contact: Bryan Pickess, "Syldata", Arne, Wareham, Dorset BH20 5BJ.

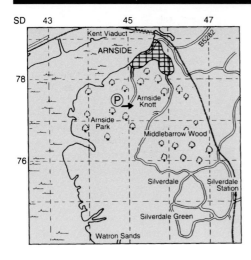

Grid Ref: SD 453 774
O.S. Map: 97

ACCESS
Public access, park in National Trust car park.

HABITAT
Broad-leaved woodland and scrub on limestone.

STATUS
National Trust owned and managed.

TARGET SPECIES
High Brown Fritillary (*Argynnis adippe*); Northern Brown Argus (*Aricia artaxerxes*); Scotch Argus (*Erebia aethiops*); Grayling (*Hipparchia semele*).

TIMING
June week 2 to July week 2 for Northern Brown Argus, June week 4 to July week 4 for High Brown Fritillary. A visit in July week 1 or 2 is recommended to connect with both target species. July week 4 to August week 2 for Scotch Argus and Grayling.

OTHER SPECIES
Most of the typical northern woodland and grassland butterfly species can be seen at this site.

OTHER FLORA AND FAUNA
The site supports several woodland bird species and has a woodland ground flora typical of limestone.

OTHER INFORMATION
A visit to this site could be combined with other limestone pavement sites such as Warton Crag, Gait Barrows and Whitbarrow Scar.

ACCESS IS STRICTLY BY PERMIT ONLY. THE YORKSHIRE WILDLIFE TRUST WILL ISSUE DIRECTIONS TO THE SITE WITH THE PERMIT

ACCESS
Permit only.

HABITAT
Moist grassland with broadleaved woodland on the valley slopes.

STATUS
Yorkshire Wildlife Trust Nature Reserve.

TARGET SPECIES
Duke of Burgundy (*Hamearis lucina*).

TIMING
May week 3 to June week 2.

OTHER SPECIES
Many common grassland and woodland butterfly species occur.

OTHER FLORA AND FAUNA
Birdseye Primrose, Globeflower, Grass of Parnassus and Marsh Lousewort are present. Fifty-five bird species have been recorded and Red, Fallow and Roe Deer occur.

OTHER INFORMATION
To avoid trampling the ground flora, please keep to the footpaths. A permit to visit this site must be obtained from Yorkshire Wildlife Trust, 10 Toft Green, York, YO1 1JT

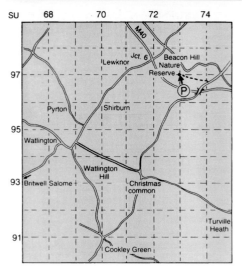

Grid Ref: SU 730 970
O.S. Map: 165

ACCESS
Open access. Park in reserve car park and walk down the hill to the meadow areas.

HABITAT
Chalk grassland, scrub and woodland.

STATUS
National Nature Reserve, owned and managed by English Nature.

TARGET SPECIES
Silver-spotted Skipper (*Hesperia comma*); Chalkhill Blue (*Lysandra coridon*); Brown Argus (*Aricia agestis*).

TIMING
All May and August week 2 to September week 1 for Brown Argus, July week 4 to August week 4 for Chalkhill Blue, August weeks 2 to 4 for Silver-spotted Skipper.

OTHER SPECIES
Many common butterfly species can be encountered.

OTHER FLORA AND FAUNA
A wide range of calcareous plant species are present. Introduced Red Kite common in the area.

OTHER INFORMATION
A visit to this site can be combined with a visit to Watlington Hill.

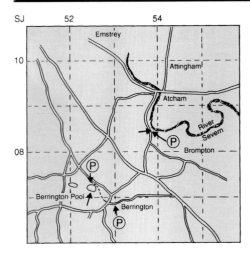

Grid Ref: SJ 538 084 - ATCHAM
SJ 526 073 - BERRINGTON POOL
O.S. Map: 126

ACCESS
Public access to both sites. Park as
indicated on map.

HABITAT
Atcham - well vegetated bank of the
River Severn; Berrington Pool is a
large pool with rich waterside
vegetation.

TARGET SPECIES
Atcham - White-legged Damselfly (*Platycnemis pennipes*); Banded Demoiselle
(*Calopteryx splendens*); Club-tailed Dragonfly (*Gomphus vulgatissimus*). Berrington Pool -
Downy Emerald (*Cordulia aenea*); Variable Damselfly (*Coenagrion pulchellum*); Red-eyed
Damselfly (*Erythromma najas*).

TIMING
June week 2 prior to fishing season if possible.

OTHER SPECIES
Many common damselflies occur at Berrington Pool.

OTHER INFORMATION
Attain Berrington Pool by the public footpath. Atcham site is at the car park by the River
Severn.

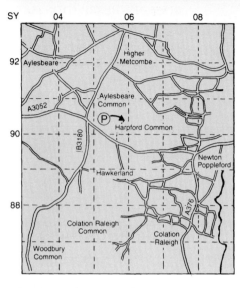

Grid Ref: SY 057 898
(access to car park from road)
O.S. Map: 192

ACCESS
Public access to nature trail only.
Park at SY 059 903.

HABITAT
Dry and wet heath.

STATUS
RSPB Nature Reserve, SSSI.

TARGET SPECIES
Southern Damselfly (*Coenagrion mercuriale*); Keeled Skimmer (*Orthetrum coerulescens*).

TIMING
July for Southern Damselfly, June week 1 to July week 3 for Keeled Skimmer.

OTHER SPECIES
Twenty-two species of dragonfly have been recorded, 16 of which have bred. Migrant Hawker (*Aeshna mixta*) and Hairy Dragonfly (*Brachytron pratense*) are amongst the dragonflies recorded. Over 35 species of butterfly have been recorded including Wood White (*Leptidea sinapis*) and six species of Fritillary although only Pearl-bordered (*Boloria euphrosyne*), Small Pearl-bordered (*Boloria selene*), Silver-washed (*Argynnis paphia*) and Dark Green (*Argynnis aglaja*) breed.

OTHER FLORA AND FAUNA
Dartford Warbler, Hobby, Stonechat and other heathland species.

OTHER INFORMATION
Contact: Pete Gotham, Mount Pleasant, Stoneyford, Colaton Raleigh, Devon EX10 0HZ.

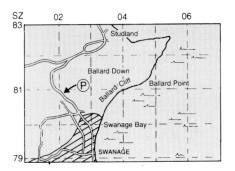

Grid Ref: SZ 029 809
O.S. Map: 195

ACCESS
Public access along footpaths.
Park in lay-by as indicated on map.

HABITAT
Chalk downland with scattered gorse
and scrub.

STATUS
Owned by National Trust.

TARGET SPECIES
Lulworth Skipper (*Thymelicus acteon*); Dingy Skipper (*Erynnis tages*); Chalkhill Blue
(*Lysandra coridon*); Adonis Blue (*Lysandra bellargus*); Marbled White (*Melanargia
galathea*).

TIMING
A visit between July week 4 and August week 3 is recommended to enable most species to
be seen. Mid-August best for Adonis Blue.

OTHER SPECIES
Brown Argus (*Aricia agestis*), Dark Green Fritillary (*Argynnis aglaja*), Clouded Yellow
(*Colias croceus*) and many common species.

OTHER FLORA AND FAUNA
The area contains many calcareous plant species and is also important for grasshoppers
and crickets. Dartford Warbler.

OTHER INFORMATION
Lulworth Skipper can be found on many of the headlands and coves along the coast. It is
possible to combine this visit with a trip to Durlston Country Park or a beach day with the
family!

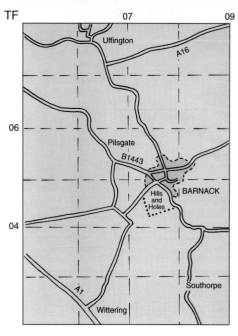

Grid Ref: TF 075 046
O.S. Map: 142

ACCESS
Open, with four parking places on the perimeter roads.

HABITAT
Limestone grassland over a hummocky ancient quarry site.

STATUS
National Nature Reserve managed by English Nature.

TARGET SPECIES
Brown Argus (*Aricia agestis*); Marbled White (*Melanargia galathea*); Chalkhill Blue (*Lysandra coridon*); Essex Skipper (*Thymelicus lineola*).

TIMING
May weeks 2 to 4 for first brood Brown Argus; all July Marbled White; August weeks 1 to 3 for Chalkhill Blue, Essex Skipper and second brood Brown Argus.

OTHER SPECIES
Many other common species occur.

OTHER FLORA AND FAUNA
Good site for Glow-worm. Abundant Man Orchid plus other orchids including Frog. Large colony of Knapweed Broomrape. Pasque Flower in flower in April.

OTHER INFORMATION
Its proximity to the A1 makes it an ideal stopping-off point. Brown Argus and Marbled White colonies are strong.

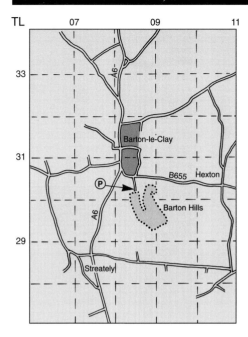

Grid Ref: TL 085 303
O.S. Map: 166

ACCESS
From Church Road at Barton-le-Clay.
Park carefully not causing obstruction.
Open access.

HABITAT
Valley with steep sided hills, chalk
grassland and woodland.

STATUS
National Nature Reserve, managed by
English Nature, within the Chilterns
Area of Outstanding Natural Beauty.

TARGET SPECIES
Dingy Skipper (*Erynnis tages*); Brown
Argus (*Aricia agestis*); Chalkhill Blue
(*Lysandra coridon*); Marbled White
(*Melanargia galathea*); White-letter
Hairstreak (*Strymonidia
w-album*).

TIMING
May week 3 to June week 2 for Dingy Skipper and first brood Brown Argus. July weeks 1
to 3 for Marbled White and White-letter Hairstreak. August weeks 2 to 4 for second brood
Brown Argus and Chalkhill Blue.

OTHER SPECIES
Twenty-six species regularly recorded each year.

OTHER FLORA AND FAUNA
Pasque Flower in Spring and Hobby regularly recorded. This reserve has 10% of
Bedfordshire's chalk grassland and has a wide range of plants typical of the habitat
including seven orchid species.

OTHER INFORMATION
If a group visit is intended notify the very helpful site manager Graham Bellamy,
Tel: 01462 711371. A visit could be combined with Sewell Cutting or Whipsnade and
Dunstable Downs. This latter area has similar species plus Grizzled Skipper (*Pyrgus
malvae*) and Duke of Burgundy (*Hamearis lucina*). This hard to work area can be accessed
at TL 008 198.

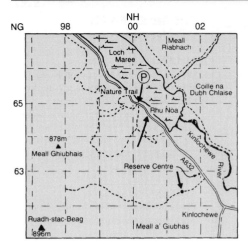

Grid Ref: NH 004 647
O.S. Map: 19

ACCESS
Park at NH 001 650.

HABITAT
Open boggy clearings.

STATUS
National Nature Reserve.

TARGET SPECIES
Northern Emerald (*Somatachlora arctica*); Black Darter (*Sympetrum danea*); Golden-ringed Dragonfly (*Cordulegaster boltonii*).

TIMING
June week 4 to July week 4 for Golden-ringed Dragonfly; all July for Northern Emerald; July week 3 to August week 4 for Black Darter.

OTHER SPECIES
It is possible to see 13 species of dragonfly in the vicinity in a day, but it is hard work. Large Heath (*Coenonympha tullia*) in small numbers.

OTHER FLORA AND FAUNA
Creeping Lady's Tresses are scattered and other Scottish orchid species are present.

OTHER INFORMATION
Wellingtons are essential for this site. A visit to this site should be combined with one to Bridge of Grudie.

The Pony Track at NH 014 624 is also worth exploring. Park at the Reserve Centre. In the unlikely event of missing Northern Emerald at this site try Coire Loch in Glen Affric, O.S. Map: 25 at NH 294 283.

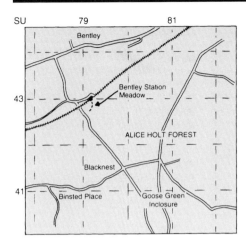

Grid Ref: SU 794 428
O.S. Map: 186

ACCESS
On the A31 Guildford-Alton Road, turn at Bentley Village for Bentley Station. The reserve is 100m south-east of Bentley Station car park. Public access.

HABITAT
A sheltered herb-rich meadow, alongside an oakwood.

STATUS
Butterfly Conservation Nature Reserve.

TARGET SPECIES
Purple Emperor (*Apatura iris*); Purple Hairstreak (*Quercusia quercus*); Silver-washed Fritillary (*Argynnis paphia*); White Admiral (*Ladoga camilla*); Grizzled Skipper (*Pyrgus malvae*).

TIMING
May week 2 to June week 1 for Grizzled Skipper, July weeks 2 and 3 for other target species bar Purple Hairstreak which is July week 4 to August week 3.

OTHER SPECIES
Many other common butterfly species occur.

OTHER FLORA AND FAUNA
Plants include Spiny Restharrow and Pepper Saxifrage.

OTHER INFORMATION
Purple Emperor is not easy at this site.

Contact: Ken Willmott, 3 Yarm Court Road, Leatherhead, Surrey KT22 8NY.

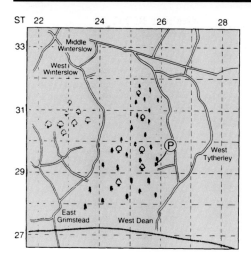

Grid Ref: ST 259 292

O.S. Map: 184

ACCESS
Public access along woodland rides and footpaths.

HABITAT
Mixed woodland with open glades and rides.

STATUS
Forest Enterprise managed woodland.

TARGET SPECIES
Purple Emperor (*Apatura iris*); Purple Hairstreak (*Quercusia quercus*); White-letter Hairstreak (*Strymonidia w-album*). The latter may prove difficult.

TIMING
July weeks 2 and 3 for Purple Emperor and White-letter Hairstreak, July week 4 to August week 2 for Purple Hairstreak.

OTHER SPECIES
Also occurring are White Admiral (*Ladoga camilla*); Ringlet (*Apantopus hyperantus*); Marbled White (*Melanargia galathea*); Brown Argus (*Aricia agestis*) and five species of Fritillary, although High Brown (*Argynnis adippe*) and Dark Green (*Argynnis aglaja*) are not as common as Pearl-bordered (*Boloria euphrosyne*), Small Pearl-bordered (*Boloria selene*) or Silver-washed (*Argynnis paphia*). Twenty species can be recorded in a July visit.

OTHER FLORA AND FAUNA
Nightingales are amongst the many woodland species of bird that can be heard or seen in the wood. There is a typical woodland ground flora in the broad-leaved sections.

OTHER INFORMATION
The good area for seeing Purple Emperors in some years is around the car park; they come down from the canopy in the late morning to feed on rotting fruit put out for them. It is worth spending a full day exploring the area, but if forestry operations are being undertaken, do not enter any cordoned off areas. Be on site no later than 10 am for Purple Emperor at its finest location in Britain.

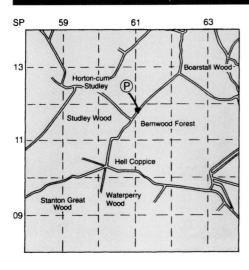

Grid Ref: SP 611 117
O.S. Map: 164

ACCESS
Open access, but keep to the rides.

HABITAT
Mixed woodland with broad, well-vegetated rides.

STATUS
Forest Enterprise woodland.

TARGET SPECIES
Black Hairstreak (*Strymonidia pruni*);
Brown Hairstreak (*Thecla betulae*) and
White Admiral (*Ladoga camilla*).

TIMING
June week 4 and July week 1 for Black Hairstreak, July for White Admiral, August weeks 2 to 4 for Brown Hairstreak.

OTHER SPECIES
Most common woodland species have been recorded. Forty butterfly species have bred on the reserve, but a single visit is only likely to produce half this number.

OTHER FLORA AND FAUNA
Most common woodland birds can be expected. Green-winged Orchid occurs.

OTHER INFORMATION
The best area for Black and Brown Hairstreak is in the Blackthorn at SP 610 110. Bernwood has deteriorated for Purple Emperor.

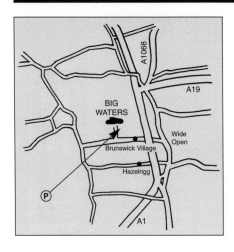

Grid Ref: NZ 227 734
O.S. Map: 88

ACCESS
Open access. From the B1318 in Wide Open, turn west at the Traveller's Rest Public House. Go under the A1 flyover and through Brunswick Village, turn north just beyond Emmerson's Hotel and park in the car park at the end of the road.

HABITAT
Large subsidence pond surrounded by Carr woodland and Birch and Alder plantation.

STATUS
Northumberland Wildlife Trust nature reserve. SSSI.

TARGET SPECIES
Banded Demoiselle (*Calopteryx splendens*) at Belasis Bridge on the nearby River Blyth.

TIMING
From June week 2 and all July.

OTHER SPECIES
Considered the best Northumberland Wildlife Trust Reserve for butterflies and dragonflies. Eight species of *Odonata* breed.

OTHER FLORA AND FAUNA
During the winter, the feeding stations attract wintering woodland and farmland birds such as Tree Sparrow and Great Spotted Woodpecker. Great Crested and Little Grebes, Common Tern and Sedge Warbler breed.

OTHER INFORMATION
Contact: Northumberland Wildlife Trust, The Garden House, St Nicholas Park, Jubilee Road, Newcastle-upon-Tyne NE3 3XT.

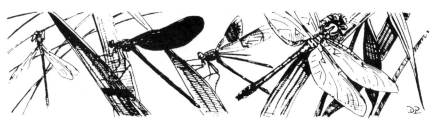

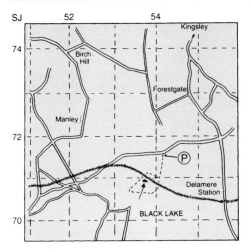

Grid Ref: SJ 537 709
O.S. Map: 117

ACCESS
Public access. Park at Barnsbridge Gate car park (SJ 542 715) on the south side of the Mouldsworth/Hatchmere road. Follow the public footpath south through the forest over the railway line.

HABITAT
A small acidic lake surrounded by trees, with a partial carpet of Sphagnum Moss.

STATUS
Cheshire Wildlife Trust Nature Reserve, SSSI. The area is part of the Forest Enterprise owned Delamere Forest.

TARGET SPECIES
White-faced Darter (*Leucorrhinia dubia*); Black Darter (*Sympetrum danea*); Common Hawker (*Aeshna juncea*).

TIMING
June week 1 to July week 1 for White-faced Darter. August for Common Hawker and Black Darter.

OTHER SPECIES
Many common species of dragonfly and damselfly occur at this site. Several species of common butterfly can be seen and Small Pearl-bordered Fritillary (*Boloria selene*) survives in small numbers at three sites within the forest.

OTHER FLORA AND FAUNA
Many common woodland birds occur including Siskin and Pied Flycatcher.

OTHER INFORMATION
View the lake only from the surrounding footpath. On no account venture on to the floating vegetation. Take binoculars and/or telescope for good views.

Contact: Cheshire Wildlife Trust, Grebe House, Reaseheath, Nantwich, Cheshire CW5 6DA.

23

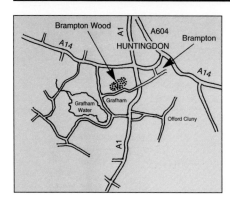

Grid Ref: TL 185 698
O.S. Map: 153

ACCESS
Open access, but visitors are requested to keep to the paths and rides. The reserve is on the north side of the road which runs between Grafham village and Brampton, and is nearly 2 kms west of the A1. Take the A1 south and exit at Brampton Hut roundabout towards Huntingdon, then turn right into Brampton and right again into Grafham Road.

HABITAT
The reserve is ancient woodland containing Ash, Field Maple and Hazel. There are dense thickets of Blackthorn.

STATUS
SSSI.

TARGET SPECIES
Black Hairstreak (*Strymonidia pruni*); White Admiral (*Ladoga camilla*); White-letter Hairstreak (*Strymonidia w-album*); Purple Hairstreak (*Quercusia quercus*).

TIMING
June week 4 to July week 1 for Black Hairstreak; July weeks 1 to 3 for White-letter Hairstreak and White Admiral; July week 3 to August week 1 for Purple Hairstreak.

OTHER SPECIES
Twenty-nine species of butterfly have been recorded.

OTHER FLORA AND FAUNA
Good flora including False Oxslip. All three woodpeckers present.

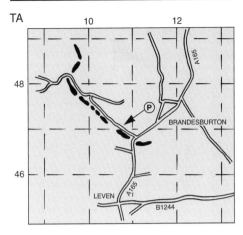

Grid Ref: TA 105 470 (parking)
O.S. Map: 107

ACCESS
Public access, off the A165 1km south
of Brandesburton village.

HABITAT
A series of angling ponds.

TARGET SPECIES
Red-eyed Damselfly (*Erythromma najas*).

TIMING
A visit during June or July will connect with the target species, although an early June visit
avoids the angling season.

OTHER SPECIES
Many common damsel and dragonfly species occur.

OTHER FLORA AND FAUNA
Small numbers of wildfowl occur on the ponds and common warblers frequent the
surrounding vegetation.

OTHER INFORMATION
A visit here could be combined with a trip to Hornsea Mere or Bempton Cliffs for birds.
The target species is on the northern edge of its range at this site.

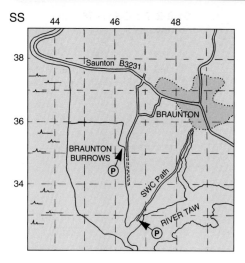

Grid Ref: SS 4535 (general area)
O.S. Map: 180

ACCESS
Open. Car parks at SS 463 352 and SS 466 327.

HABITAT
Coastal dune system.

STATUS
International Biosphere Reserve and SSSI.

TARGET SPECIES
Grizzled Skipper (*Pyrgus malvae*); Dingy Skipper (*Erynnis tages*); Small Blue (*Cupido minimus*); Marbled White (*Melanargia galathea*); Dark Green Fritillary (*Argynnis aglaja*); Grayling (*Hipparchia semele*).

TIMING
May week 4 to June week 2 for Grizzled Skipper, Dingy Skipper and Small Blue; July weeks 2 to 4 for Marbled White, Dark Green Fritillary and Grayling.

OTHER SPECIES
Thirty-three butterfly and 14 damsel and dragonfly species have been recorded.

OTHER FLORA AND FAUNA
Over 400 species of flowering plants including marsh orchids and Marsh Helleborine in large numbers.

OTHER INFORMATION
A gigantic area of 604 ha. Part is used by the military. No access to those areas when the red flags are flying.

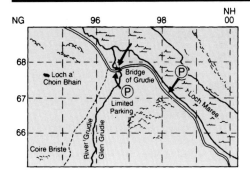

Grid Ref: NG 965 678
O.S. Map: 19

ACCESS
Limited parking at above reference or at NG 982 671. Road verges are very soft, so park with care.

HABITAT
Open boggy clearings.

TARGET SPECIES
Northern Emerald (*Somatachlora arctica*); Black Darter (*Sympetrum danae*); Highland Darter (*Sympetrum nigrescens*); Golden-ringed Dragonfly (*Cordulegaster boltonii*); Azure Hawker (*Aeshna caerulea*) possible.

TIMING
Azure Hawker, June week 4 to July week 2. Northern Emerald throughout July. Golden-ringed, June week 2 to July week 4. Black and Highland Darter, July week 4 to August week 4.

OTHER SPECIES
Large Heath (*Coenonympha tullia*) in small numbers.

OTHER FLORA AND FAUNA
Creeping Lady's Tresses and other orchids scattered.

OTHER INFORMATION
Wellingtons essential. Check the boggy clearings immediately north of the bridge.

Combine this site with the nearby Beinn Eighe National Nature Reserve.

NX   36

75

A714

To Newton
Stewart

Grid Ref: NX 359 754
O.S. Map: 77

ACCESS
Directly adjacent to small parking area at roadside.

HABITAT
Flooded quarry in conifer clearing. Small areas of scrub and grassy rides.

STATUS
Conservation area managed by Forest Enterprise.

TARGET SPECIES
Ten species of *Odonata,* including Common Hawker (*Aeshna juncea*); Golden-ringed Dragonfly (*Cordulegaster boltonii*) and Black Darter (*Sympetrum danae*).

TIMING
Late July and August.

OTHER SPECIES
Scotch Argus (*Erebia aethiops*); Ringlet (*Aphantopus hyperantus*); Small Pearl-bordered Fritillary (*Boloria selene*).

OTHER INFORMATION
Within the Galloway Forest Park, where many similar sites can be explored. Can be combined with visit to Wood of Cree.

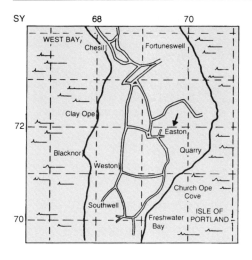

Grid Ref: SY 697 720
O.S. Map: 194

ACCESS
Take the A354 to Portland and follow signs for Easton. Turn left into Grove Road and then turn right into the car park. Follow the footpath east to the quarry.

HABITAT
Disused limestone quarry, filled and capped with calcareous soil.

STATUS
Butterfly Conservation Nature Reserve.

TARGET SPECIES
Silver-studded Blue (*Plebejus argus* ssp. *cretaceus*); Small Blue (*Cupido minimus*) and Dark Green Fritillary (*Argynnis aglaja*).

TIMING
May week 4 to June week 3 for Small Blue, July week 3 to August week 1 for Silver-studded Blue and Dark Green Fritillary.

OTHER SPECIES
Several other common butterfly species occur.

OTHER FLORA AND FAUNA
Bee and Pyramidal Orchids, Yellow Vetching, Autumn Gentian and Ivy Broomrape.

OTHER INFORMATION
Contact: Robert Smith, Hooke Springs Cottage, Hooke, Beaminster, Dorset DT8 3NZ.

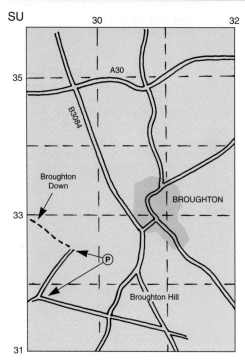

Grid Ref: SU 292 329
O.S. Map: 185

ACCESS
Open. Drive along flinty and bumpy track from the road to the south to SU 296 326 or park carefully along the road and walk the track so avoiding possible burst tyres.

HABITAT
Chalk downland, scrub and woodland.

STATUS
Hampshire Wildlife Trust Reserve.

TARGET SPECIES
Duke of Burgundy (*Hamearis lucina*); Brown Argus (*Aricia agestis*); Chalkhill Blue (*Lysandra coridon*); Silver-spotted Skipper (*Hesperia comma*).

TIMING
May week 3 to June week 1 for Duke of Burgundy and first brood Brown Argus; August weeks 2 to 4 for second brood Brown Argus, Chalkhill Blue and Silver-spotted Skipper.

OTHER SPECIES
Many other common species occur.

OTHER FLORA AND FAUNA
A wide range of chalk downland plants are present.

OTHER INFORMATION
Nearby, Stockbridge Down at SU 374 347 has a large population of Chalkhill Blue, plus Dark Green Fritillary and Brown Argus.

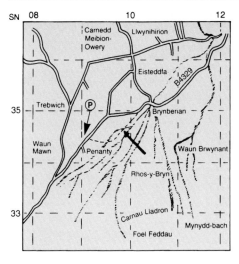

Grid Ref: SN 099 347
O.S. Map: 145

ACCESS
Open public access, but keep to paths. Park along road, but avoid damage to verge and blocking entrances. Access path from SN 092 344.

HABITAT
A series of streams on moorland.

TARGET SPECIES
Southern Damselfly (*Coenagrion mercuriale*); Keeled Skimmer (*Orthetrum coerulescens*); Golden-ringed Dragonfly (*Cordulegaster boltonii*).

TIMING
The target species are all on the wing from June week 4 to July week 4.

OTHER SPECIES
Small Red Damselfly (*Ceriagrion tenellum*) and Scarce Blue-tailed Damselfly (*Ishnura pumilio*) have been recorded in the past.

OTHER FLORA AND FAUNA
Typical flora for the area can be found.

OTHER INFORMATION
As the site can get very wet, wellingtons are recommended.

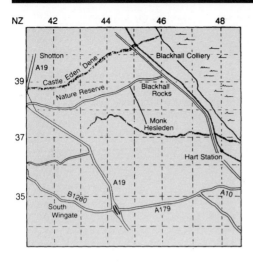

Grid Ref: NZ 410 387
O.S. Map: 88 and 93

ACCESS
Public access from the A19.

HABITAT
Mixed woodland along the steep banks of the River Dene with glades and clearings.

STATUS
National Nature Reserve, owned and managed by English Nature.

TARGET SPECIES
Northern Brown Argus (*Aricia artaxerxes* ssp *salmacis*).

TIMING
June week 2 to July week 2.

OTHER SPECIES
Many common butterfly species may be encountered.

OTHER FLORA AND FAUNA
The area has a rich and varied flora including several species of wild geranium such as Meadow, Bloody and Wood-cranesbill. Giant Bellflower, Fly and Birdsnest Orchid occur. In the wetter places Marsh Arrowgrass and Dame's Violet grow. Typical woodland birds occur, whilst the coastal area may attract migrant waders and terns.

OTHER INFORMATION
The Northern Brown Argus at this site is the subspecies known as Castle Eden Argus. A full day could easily be spent exploring this varied site, especially if combining several natural history pursuits.

Further information from English Nature, Oakerside Dene Lodge, Stanhope Chase, Peterlee, County Durham SR8 1NJ.

Yellow-winged Darter — *Amazing numbers of this rare migrant were seen throughout England and Wales in 1995.* (Colin Twist)

Black Lake — *Site for White-faced Darter.* (Colin Twist)

Arnside Knott — *Home for High Brown Fritillary in Cumbria.* (Colin Twist)

High Brown Fritillary — *A declining species in Britain.* (Colin Twist)

White Admiral — *A butterfly of woodlands in the Midlands and the South of England.*   (Colin Twist)

Marsh Fritillary — *A species threatened by habitat destruction in Britain.*   (Paul M. Hill)

Scarce Emerald Damselfly — *Confined to just a handful of sites in England and believed extinct until recently rediscovered.* (Colin Twist)

Brimstone — *A regularly occurring species in southern Britain.* (Paul M. Hill)

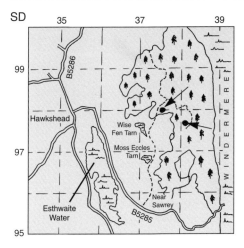

Grid Ref: SD 382 976
O.S. Map: 96 or 97

ACCESS
Open. Access along bridleway and forest tracks from Near Sawrey SD 371 957.

HABITAT
Acidic pool in woodland.

STATUS
Unknown.

TARGET SPECIES
Downy Emerald (*Cordulia aenea*); White-faced Darter (*Leucorrhinia dubia*); Golden-ringed Dragonfly (*Corduligaster boltonii*).

TIMING
June week 2 to July week 1 for all species.

OTHER SPECIES
A good cross-section of other *Odonata* are present. Small Pearl-bordered Fritillary *(Boloria selene)* is also found.

OTHER FLORA AND FAUNA
Red Squirrel, Red Deer and hill birds including Common Buzzard are regularly seen. Outside the breeding season the area is a notable Raven roost.

OTHER INFORMATION
The walk is over one hour from Near Sawrey, not strenuous, but walking shoes or boots should be worn. The tarn at SD 375 980 is worth checking for *Odonata*.

An up-to-date O.S. Map for the area must be used for this site.

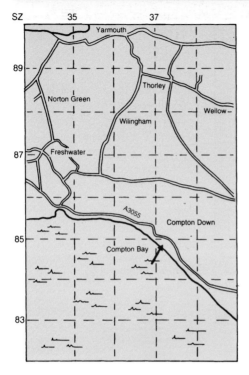

Grid Ref: SZ 372 848
O.S. Map: 196

ACCESS
Open access to the undercliff below the A3055.

HABITAT
Crumbling undercliff on the coastline.

TARGET SPECIES
Glanville Fritillary (*Melitaea cinxia*).

TIMING
June weeks 1 to 3 for Glanville Fritillary.

OTHER SPECIES
Other common butterfly species can be seen. Adonis Blue (*Lysandra bellargus*) and Small Blue (*Cupido minimus*) have been recorded on Compton Down.

OTHER FLORA AND FAUNA
Hoary Stock and Bee Orchid grow nearby.

OTHER INFORMATION
It is possible to visit this site by taking the ferry (as a foot passenger) from Lymington to Yarmouth and completing the journey by bus. Similar habitats at St. Catherine's Point and Luccombe Chine either side of Ventnor are worth checking for Glanville Fritillary.

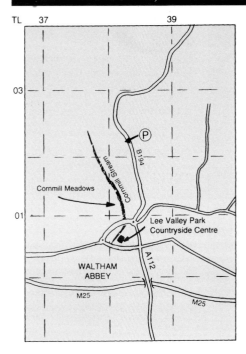

Grid Ref: TL 380 013
O.S. Map: 166

ACCESS
Public access. Approach from the Cornmill Meadows car park off the B194 or the Lee Valley Park Countryside Centre.

HABITAT
Mixed habitat with slow flowing watercourses.

STATUS
Country Park.

TARGET SPECIES
White-legged Damselfly (*Platcnemis pennipes*); Red-eyed Damselfly (*Erythromma najas*); Banded Demoiselle (*Calopteryx splendens*); Hairy Dragonfly (*Brachytron pratense*); Migrant Hawker (*Aeshna mixta*) and Emperor Dragonfly (*Anax imperator*).

TIMING
May weeks 2 to 4 for Hairy Dragonfly, June week 3 to July week 3 for White-legged and Red-eyed Damselflies, Banded Demoiselle and Emperor. August week 2 to September week 3 for Migrant Hawker.

OTHER SPECIES
Eighteen species of dragonfly are regularly recorded. Essex Skipper (*Thymelicus lineola*) is amongst the various butterfly species recorded.

OTHER INFORMATION
Regarded by many as the best dragonfly site in Greater London, Essex and Hertfordshire.

There is a Countryside Centre and car parking at Waltham Abbey, adjacent to the Dragonfly Sanctuary. The descriptive leaflet produced is one of the finest the authors have seen.

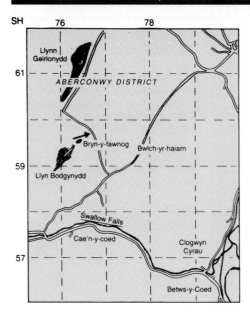

Grid Ref: SH 767 597
O.S. Map: 115

ACCESS
Open access. The site is on the west side of the minor road, 1km south of Llyn Geirionydd.

HABITAT
Moorland bog.

TARGET SPECIES
Keeled Skimmer (*Orthetrum coerulescens*).

TIMING
Throughout July.

OTHER SPECIES
Four-spotted Chaser (*Libellula quadrimaculata*) and common damselflies.

OTHER FLORA AND FAUNA
The adjacent woodland contains many typical woodland bird species, whilst Dipper and Grey Wagtail can be seen along the streams.

OTHER INFORMATION
A visit to this site could be combined with one to the Great Orme, Llandudno.

The RSPB have recently opened a new nature reserve on the Conwy, with access off the A55.

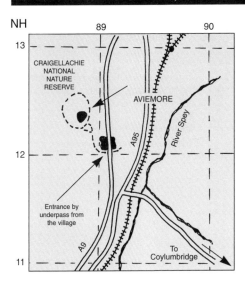

Grid Ref: NH 892 121 (access via underpass)
O.S. Map: 36

ACCESS
Open. Via an underpass beneath the A9 located near the dry ski slope at the Aviemore Mountain Resort. Follow marked trails, concentrating particularly on the pools.

HABITAT
Birch woodland, cliff and moorland.

STATUS
National Nature Reserve.

TARGET SPECIES
Highland Darter (*Sympetrum nigrescens*).

TIMING
All August to September week 2.

OTHER SPECIES
Common northern species of butterflies and *Odonata* occur.

OTHER FLORA AND FAUNA
Peregrine, Grouse and typical woodland birds occur. Good moths, some of a very local distribution. Roe Deer are present.

OTHER INFORMATION
Four kilometres away to the south, Loch an Eilein holds Highland Darter and other species. NH 897 087 for parking (fee). A path does a circuit of the loch.

The boggy ground adjacent to the B970 at NH 955193 is said to hold northern specialities but showed little on two visits by CT. Still worth checking in sunny weather.

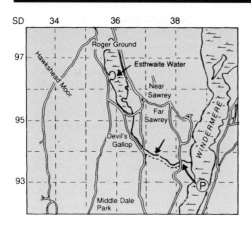

Grid Ref: SD 374 938
O.S. Map: 97

ACCESS
Park at SD 382 935 and follow public footpath along the beck.

HABITAT
Well vegetated stream running from Esthwaite Water to Windermere.

TARGET SPECIES
Beautiful Demoiselle (*Calopteryx virgo*). Golden-ringed Dragonfly (*Cordulegaster boltonii*) occur spasmodically along the beck towards Esthwaite Water.

TIMING
June week 2 to July week 3.

OTHER INFORMATION
Consider combining with a visit to Grizedale Forest, where Golden-ringed Dragonfly and Four-spotted Chaser plus common damselflies occur around the pools. The Forest Centre is at SD 335 945. A visit to Whitbarrow Scar is also a possibility.

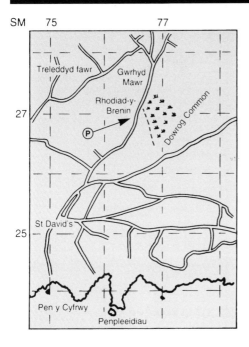

Grid Ref: SM 770 270
O.S. Map: 157

ACCESS
Public access, but keep to the paths.
Enter by path from SM 766 270.

HABITAT
Lowland bog and marshy heathland.

TARGET SPECIES
Emperor Dragonfly (*Anax imperator*);
Golden-ringed Dragonfly
(*Cordulegaster boltonii*); Beautiful
Demoiselle (*Calopteryx virgo*);
Ringlet (*Aphantopus hyperantus*).

TIMING
June week 2 to July week 4 for the
target species of dragonfly, July week
2 to August week 1 for Ringlet.

OTHER SPECIES
Many common dragonflies and damselflies occur at the site. It is possible to see ten
species in a very short visit. Several common butterfly species also occur.

OTHER FLORA AND FAUNA
Typical lowland bog plants occur such as Bog Pimpernel, Yellow Centaury and Southern
Marsh Orchid.

OTHER INFORMATION
Take care not to venture too far into the damper areas to avoid damaging the sensitive
vegetation. Wellingtons are recommended.

A visit here can be combined with a visit to Bosherton Lily Ponds parking at SR 967 947.
This open access area has a good cross-section of butterfly and dragonfly species.

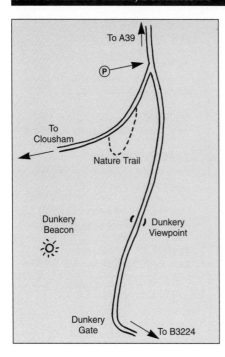

Grid Ref: SS 902 434
O.S. Map: 181

ACCESS
Open access. Park in the NT car park at SS 903 440 and walk south along the minor road towards Cloutsham, to the woodland nature trail on the left.

HABITAT
Moorland dropping down to hanging oak wood valley.

STATUS
Managed by the National Trust.

TARGET SPECIES
Heath Fritillary (*Mellicta athalia*).

TIMING
June week 4 to July week 1.

OTHER SPECIES
Many common butterflies occur.

OTHER INFORMATION
Other Heath Fritillary colonies occur in the same general area, so similar habitats are worth exploring.

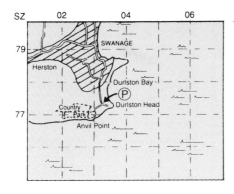

Grid Ref: SZ 033 773
O.S. Map: 195

ACCESS
Public access. Follow the signs from Swanage Town Centre and park in the pay and display car park.

HABITAT
Chalk downland with scattered scrub, some woodland and sea-cliffs.

STATUS
SSSI, Country Park.

TARGET SPECIES
Chalkhill Blue (*Lysandra coridon*); Adonis Blue (*Lysandra bellargus*); Holly Blue (*Celastrina argiolus*); Small Blue (*Cupido minimus*); Dark Green Fritillary (*Argynnis aglaja*); Marbled White (*Melanargia galathea*) and Lulworth Skipper (*Thymelicus acteon*).

TIMING
A visit between July week 3 and August week 3 is recommended to see the most species, but visits at any time in the summer will produce many butterflies. Adonis Blue is best mid-August.

OTHER SPECIES
Many common butterfly species can be encountered. Clouded Yellow (*Colias croceus*) can be seen most years.

OTHER FLORA AND FAUNA
Many calcareous plant species can be seen. Orchids include Early Spider, Pyramidal and Autumn Lady's Tresses. Nesting seabirds and passage migrants.

OTHER INFORMATION
It is possible, by prior arrangement with the rangers, to operate a moth trap on this site. Several nature trails through the various habitats are accompanied by an excellent series of leaflets about the site, obtainable from the visitor centre.

Contact: Hamish Murray, Durlston Country Park, Swanage, Dorset.

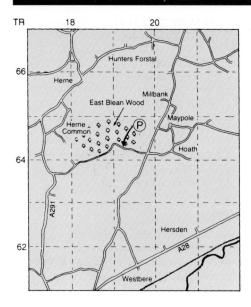

Grid Ref: TR 193 644 (Parking)
O.S. Map: 179

ACCESS
Public access, but keep to footpaths. Follow obvious paths to the north of the parking spot.

HABITAT
Woodland with mixed coppice, oak high forest and pine plantation.

STATUS
SSSI, Kent Trust for Nature Conservation Nature Reserve.

TARGET SPECIES
Heath Fritillary (*Mellicta athalia*) in good numbers.

TIMING
June week 4 to July week 2.

OTHER SPECIES
Many common woodland butterfly species have been recorded.

OTHER FLORA AND FAUNA
Typical woodland birds, including Nightingale and all three woodpeckers are present.

OTHER INFORMATION
Heath Fritillary can also be seen at the nearby Church Wood RSPB Nature Reserve which has open access. Park at TR 123 593 and explore the rides. A visit to either of these sites could be combined with the RSPB's Northward Hill Nature Reserve.

Contact: Kent Trust for Nature Conservation, PO Box 29, Maidstone, Kent ME14 1YH.

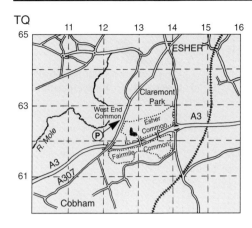

Grid Ref: TQ 125 625 (parking)
O.S. Map: 187

ACCESS
Open access.

HABITAT
Common with ponds. Adjacent Fairmile and West End Commons should also be explored.

STATUS
Common Land.

TARGET SPECIES
Brilliant Emerald (*Somatochlora metallica*); Downy Emerald (*Cordulia aenea*); White-legged Damselfly (*Platycnemis pennipes*); Red-eyed Damselfly (*Erythromma najas*).

TIMING
June week 2 to July week 4 for Red-eyed Damselfly and White-legged Damselfly. June week 1 to July week 2 for Downy Emerald and June week 4 and all July for Brilliant Emerald.

OTHER SPECIES
Banded Demoiselle (*Calopteryx splendens*) and Black-tailed Skimmer (*Orthetrum cancellatum*) also occur, plus other common species.

OTHER FLORA AND FAUNA
Common butterflies are present

OTHER INFORMATION
Middle Pond on Fairmile Common is especially good for Brilliant Emerald (TQ 127 618). Black Pond on Esher Common should also be studied (TQ 128 623) for Brilliant Emerald. Good views in 1997 here of this species. Areas adjacent to the River Mole are worthy of attention. Two footbridges over the A3 give access between the commons.

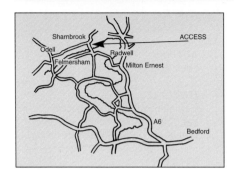

Grid Ref: SP 991 584
O.S. Map: 153

ACCESS
Take the minor road west of the A6 in Milton Ernest towards Radwell and Felmersham. Continue through the village of Felmersham, over the River Great Ouse and the reserve is located towards the 'T' junction with the Odell/Sharnbrook road. A car park is located on the western side of the road.

HABITAT
Water-filled former gravel pits with associated neutral grassland and secondary woodland.

STATUS
Site of Special Scientific Interest and Wildlife Trust nature reserve.

TARGET SPECIES
White-legged Damselfly (*Platycnemis pennipes*); Emperor Dragonfly (*Anax imperator*), Ruddy Darter (*Sympetrum sanguineum*).

TIMING
June week 3 to July week 3 for White-legged Damselfly and Emperor Dragonfly; July week 2 to August week 3 for Ruddy Darter.

OTHER SPECIES
Up to 14 other species have been recorded including Four-spotted Chaser (*Libellula quadrimaculata*), Banded Demoiselle (*Calopteryx splendens*) and Emerald Damselfly (*Lestes sponsa*).

OTHER FLORA AND FAUNA
Aquatic and marginal vegetation including Yellow Flag Iris, Purple and Yellow Loosestrifes, Yellow Water-lily and Lesser Reedmace. The site attracts a range of wildfowl and other common birds.

OTHER INFORMATION
Contact the Wildlife Trust, Priory Country Park, Barkers Lane, Bedford MK41 9SH.

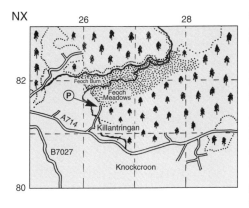

Grid Ref: NX 263 816 (parking and access point)
O.S. Map: 76

ACCESS
Open access. Care should be taken not to damage sensitive habitats.

HABITAT
Herb rich meadows on an upland farm. A stream runs the whole length of the reserve.

STATUS
Scottish Wildlife Trust Reserve.

TARGET SPECIES
Small Pearl-bordered Fritillary (*Boloria selene*); Scotch Argus (*Erebia aethiops*); Large Heath (*Coenonympha tullia*); Golden-ringed Dragonfly (*Cordulegaster boltonii*).

TIMING
All June for Small Pearl-bordered Fritillary, July weeks 1 to 3 for Large Heath, August weeks 1 to 3 for Scotch Argus, June week 3 to July week 4 for Golden-ringed Dragonfly.

OTHER SPECIES
Fourteen species of butterfly have been recorded plus several species of *Odonata*.

OTHER FLORA AND FAUNA
Good populations of Greater Butterfly and Fragrant Orchid. Small White Orchid and Frog Orchid are also present. Adder and Slow Worm have been recorded. Brown and Mountain Hare, Red and Roe Deer are occasionally seen.

OTHER INFORMATION
A visit could be combined with Auchalton Scottish Wildlife Trust Reserve, parking at the junction of the by-roads at NS 336 037. This reserve has introduced Scotch Argus and good orchid populations. Entrance to the reserve is by the parking area and there is open access.

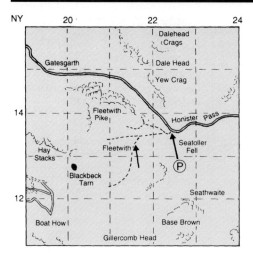

Grid Ref: NY 216 134
O.S. Map: 89

ACCESS
Park at NY 225 136 on the Honister Pass (fee) and follow the path to the site.

HABITAT
Rough, often boggy, fellside, intersected by poor footpaths.

STATUS
Part of the Lake District National Park.

TARGET SPECIES
Mountain Ringlet (*Erebia epiphron*) at one of its few and possibly most accessible English colonies.

TIMING
July weeks 1 to 3, but only attempt in good, sunny weather, as Mountain Ringlets only show in sunshine.

OTHER INFORMATION
Average fitness for the walk is required, wear strong boots or shoes and warm clothing. Take a map and food. If travelling from the south consider combining the visit with Arnside Knott, Gait Barrows, Warton Crag or Whitbarrow Scar.

Mountain Ringlet may also be encountered on other Lake District fellsides, but we feel this one is the most easily accessed.

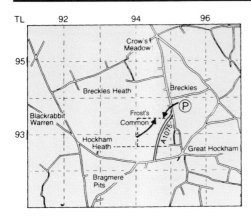

Grid Ref: TL 945 935
O.S. Map: 144

ACCESS
Public access. Park at TL 947 935 on the west side of the by-pass, 1 km north-west of Great Hockham.

HABITAT
Woodland, mainly deciduous, with rides and well vegetated pools.

TARGET SPECIES
Scarce Emerald Damselfly (*Lestes dryas*).

TIMING
Throughout July.

OTHER INFORMATION
The Scarce Emerald Damselfly has been recorded in a pool on the south side of the woodland ride at TL 945 935.

The confusion species, Emerald Damselfly also occurs, along with many common damselflies.

During the 1970's it was feared that this species, which was never very common, had become extinct in the UK, but in recent years a very small number of colonies have been discovered.

The Norfolk Wildlife Trust's Hockham Fen Reserve is nearby at TL 934 937. This remnant fen is dangerous to visit unaccompanied, but has a good range of plants and birds.

Thompson Common Norfolk Wildlife Trust Reserve not far from Frost's Common also holds Scarce Emerald Damselfly. Park at TL 934 966.

Stuart Burnet recommends a pond near Wymondham in Norfolk for Scarce Emerald Damselfly. It is at TG 124 006 on the east side of the A11 by-pass and north of the track. Adjacent ponds are also worth checking.

Contact NWT, 32 Cathedral Close, Norwich, Norfolk NR1 4DF for access information.

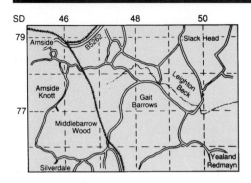

Grid Ref: SD 48 77
O.S. Map: 97

ACCESS
By permit only.

HABITAT
Limestone pavement, woodland, wetland and meadows.

STATUS
NNR owned and managed by English Nature.

TARGET SPECIES
Duke of Burgundy (*Hamearis lucina*); High Brown Fritillary (*Argynnis adippe*); Purple Hairstreak (*Quercusia quercus*).

TIMING
May week 4 to June week 2 for Duke of Burgundy, July weeks 2 to 4 for High Brown Fritillary and July week 4 to August week 3 for Purple Hairstreak.

OTHER SPECIES
Dingy Skipper (*Erynnis tages*); Pearl-bordered Fritillary (*Boloria euphrosyne*); Small Pearl-bordered Fritillary (*Boloria selene*); Northern Brown Argus (*Aricia artaxerxes*), and many other common species. Grizzled Skipper (*Pyrgus malvae*) has recently been introduced without permission.

OTHER FLORA AND FAUNA
Dark Red Helleborine, Angular Solomon's Seal, Pale St. John's Wort and Rigid Buckler Fern. The site has a large moth list and many common woodland birds for the area can be seen.

OTHER INFORMATION
Contact: Robert Petley-Jones c/o English Nature, Blackwell, Bowness-on-Windermere, Cumbria LA23 3JR. A visit to this site could be combined with the RSPB's Leighton Moss Nature Reserve or to Arnside Knott.

Beinn Eighe — *One of Scotland's premier sites for several species including Northern Emerald.*
(Colin Twist)

Highland Darter — *Female, care needs to be taken to avoid confusion with Black Darter.*
(Colin Twist)

Hairy Dragonfly — *A scarce species found along streams, dykes or canals.* (Colin Twist)

Southern Hawker — *The most inquisitive of the British* Aeshnas. *Can be found well away from water, along lanes or woodland rides.* (Julia M. Mottishaw)

Mating Silver-studded Blues — *Prees Heath in Shropshire. One of the most northerly colonies of the Silver-studded Blue in England.* (Colin Twist)

Chequered Skipper — *Although the subject of a re-introduction scheme in England, a trip to Scotland is needed to see this rare butterfly. Details of the re-introduction site are still confidential.* (Colin Twist)

Variable Damselfly — *This species has a patchy distribution. Where it occurs it can favour particular water bodies for no apparent reason.* (Colin Twist)

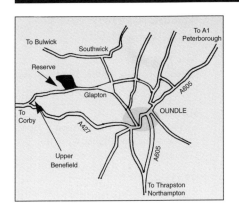

Grid Ref: TL 003 902
O.S. Map: 141

ACCESS
The reserve is on the road from Upper Benefield to Glapthorn. The village of Glapthorn is north of Oundle which can either be approached from the A605 Peterborough to Thrapston road, or from Corby via the A427. Park on grass verge alongside track opposite entrance to reserve.

HABITAT
The reserve is a mixture of woodland and dense Blackthorn scrub, intersected by grassy paths.

STATUS
SSSI.

TARGET SPECIES
Black Hairstreak (*Strymonidia pruni*).

TIMING
June week 3 to July week 1.

OTHER SPECIES
Purple Hairstreak (*Quercusia quercus*) and typical common species.

OTHER FLORA AND FAUNA
The reserve is noted for Nightingale and other summer visitors.

OTHER INFORMATION
This is one of the best-known sites for Black Hairstreak in the region.

Contact the Northampton office of the Wildlife Trust, Lings House, Billing Lings, Northampton NN3 4BE. Tel: 01604 405 285.

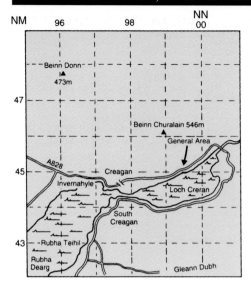

Grid Ref: NM 99 45
O.S. Map: 49 and 50

ACCESS
Contact Scottish Natural Heritage prior to visiting.

HABITAT
Mixed woodland with rides and glades, open land higher up Beinn Churalain.

STATUS
SSSI. Owned and managed by Scottish Natural Heritage.

TARGET SPECIES
Chequered Skipper (*Carterocephalus palaemon*); Small Pearl-bordered Fritillary (*Boloria selene*); Pearl-bordered Fritillary (*Boloria euphrosyne*); Dark Green Fritillary (*Argynnis aglaja*); Large Heath (*Coenonympha tullia*) and Scotch Argus (*Erebia aethiops*). Mountain Ringlet (*Erebia epiphron*) and Marsh Fritillary (*Eurodryas aurinia*) also occur.

TIMING
June weeks 1 and 2 for Chequered Skipper, Small Pearl-bordered Fritillary, Pearl-bordered Fritillary and Marsh Fritillary. July weeks 1 to 3 for Dark Green Fritillary, Large Heath and Mountain Ringlet. August weeks 1 to 3 for Scotch Argus.

OTHER SPECIES
Twenty species of butterflies have been recorded.

OTHER FLORA AND FAUNA
Many birds and plants typical of the area can be encountered on the site.

OTHER INFORMATION
This must be Scotland's No. 1 butterfly site. Check the areas under the power lines for Chequered Skipper and the fritillaries. Mountain Ringlet is on the higher slopes. Marsh Fritillary has declined here.

Contact: Scottish Natural Heritage prior to a visit. The terrain is hard and the lack of paths make the area difficult to work. Stout shoes or boots are recommended. No shorts as sheep ticks are a major problem.

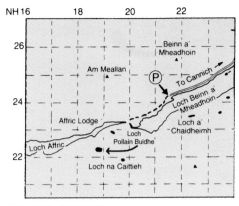

Grid Ref: NH 188 224 (Loch Pollain Buidhe)
O.S. Map: 25

ACCESS
Open access. Park at NH 216 243

HABITAT
Acidic pools, bogs and bog-pools in remnant Caledonian Pine Forest.

STATUS
Forest Enterprise managed.

TARGET SPECIES
Brilliant Emerald (*Somatachlora metallica*).

TIMING
July.

OTHER SPECIES
Fourteen species of *Odonata* breed in the Glen Affric area, but the locality is hard to work and can prove frustrating.

OTHER INFORMATION
The major target species, Brilliant Emerald occurs at several of the lochans in the area. It has been recorded on Loch Pollain Buidhe, and has been recorded on 13 other lochans in the Glen including Loch an Amair at NH 264 260 along with Downy Emerald (*Cordulia aenea*). Coire Loch at NH 294 283 may be worth checking for emeralds, with Azure Hawker and Highland Darter along nearby tracks.

Strong footwear and wet weather clothing are advised for this site.

Ability to map read is essential.

Do not attempt these sites if the weather is unreliable.

Brilliant Emerald is scarce in Scotland.

Please send all records of this, and other species seen to the Scottish recorder for BDS.

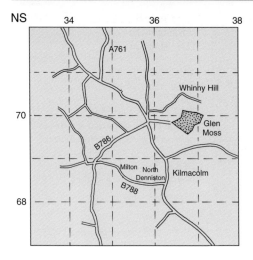

Grid Ref: NS 364 698 (access)
O.S. Map: 63

ACCESS
Open access, care must be taken not to damage fragile habitats.

HABITAT
Peatland mix of basin and valley mires with open water, grassland, heathland, scrub and woodland.

STATUS
Scottish Wildlife Trust Reserve. SSSI.

TARGET SPECIES
Azure Damselfly (*Coenagrion puella*); Black Darter (*Sympetrum danae*); Common Hawker (*Aeshna juncea*).

TIMING
June and July for Azure Damselfly and August for Black Darter and Common Hawker.

OTHER SPECIES
Eight species of *Odonata* breed.

OTHER FLORA AND FAUNA
Typical birds of the habitat occur.

OTHER INFORMATION
One of the best sites for *Odonata* in the area. Azure Damselfly is towards the northern edge of its range.

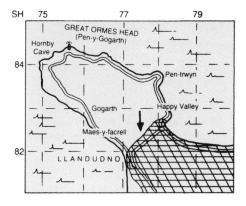

Grid Ref: SH 77 83
O.S. Map: 115

ACCESS
Public access to most of the area.

HABITAT
Open grassland on carboniferous limestone. Sea-cliffs.

STATUS
Country Park and Local Nature Reserve.

TARGET SPECIES
Silver-studded Blue (*Plebejus argus* ssp *caernensis*); Grayling (*Hipparchia semele* ssp *thyone*).

TIMING
June week 2 to July week 3 for Silver-studded Blue which flies earlier than its southern counterparts. July week 1 to August week 4 for Grayling.

OTHER SPECIES
Several of the commoner butterfly species can be seen on the Orme. There are occasional records of Dark Green Fritillary (*Argynnis aglaja*).

OTHER FLORA AND FAUNA
Guillemots, Razorbills and Fulmars nest on the sea-cliffs. During migration periods Gannets, skuas and shearwaters can be seen offshore and passerine migrants rest on the Orme. Calcicole flora includes Wild Cabbage, Hoary and Common Rock Roses, Spring Squill, Bloody Cranesbill and a number of national rarities.

OTHER INFORMATION
There is a visitor centre at the Country Park, where an information board contains details of recent sightings. The steep slopes immediately above the town should be checked first around SH 774 825. A trip here could be combined with one to the Welsh Mountain Zoo at Conwy, or to Cors Bodgynydd.

61

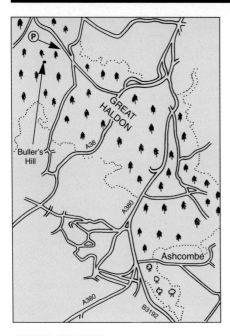

Grid Ref: SX 884 848 (Buller's Hill car park)
O.S. Map: 192

ACCESS
Public access.

HABITAT
Conifer plantations with small stands of deciduous trees. Open clearings and heathland.

STATUS
The woodlands belong to Forest Enterprise.

TARGET SPECIES
Wood White (*Leptidea sinapis*) High Brown Fritillary (*Argynnis adippe*).

TIMING
May week 3 to June week 3 for Wood White, all July for High Brown Fritillary.

OTHER SPECIES
Thirty-five species of butterfly have been recorded within the forest including Grizzled Skipper (*Pyrgus malvae*) and White Admiral (*Ladoga camilla*).

OTHER FLORA AND FAUNA
The area supports several birds of prey including Honey Buzzard, Hobby and Goshawk – all best seen from the Bird of Prey Viewpoint. Plants include Greater Butterfly Orchid and Common Spotted Orchid.

OTHER INFORMATION
The 'Butterfly Walks' at the northern end of the site, follow cleared glades under the power lines. A series of leaflets about the site are available at the Forest Enterprise offices at Buller's Hill. Contact: Forest Enterprise, Buller's Hill, Great Haldon Wood, Devon.

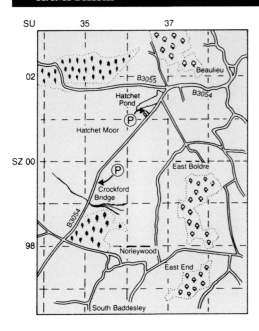

Grid Ref: SU 365 012 HATCHET POND
SZ 351 990 - CROCKFORD BRIDGE
O.S. Map: 195

ACCESS
Public access.

HABITAT
Well vegetated stream and ponds surrounded by lowland heath at Hatchet and by scrub at Crockford.

STATUS
Part of the New Forest National Park.

TARGET SPECIES
Small Red Damselfly (*Ceriagrion tenellum*); Red-eyed Damselfly (*Erythromma najas*); Southern Damselfly (*Coenagrion mercuriale*); Emperor Dragonfly (*Anax imperator*); Silver-studded Blue (*Plebejus argus*); Grayling (*Hipparchia semele*).

TIMING
June week 4 to August week 1 is recommended to see most of the target species.

OTHER SPECIES
Most common, southern dragonflies and damselflies can be encountered. Purple Hairstreak (*Quercusia quercus*) can be seen in the oaks at Crockford Bridge.

OTHER FLORA AND FAUNA
Hobbies may be seen hunting over the heathland. Common Lizard.

OTHER INFORMATION
The Southern Damselflies wander quite far along the stream away from Crockford Bridge into the heathland itself. The other species can be seen at Hatchet Pond.

Take care when crossing the main road at Crockford Bridge.

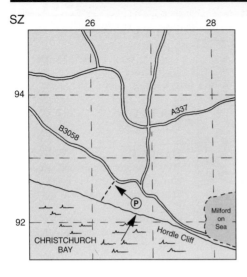

Grid Ref: SZ 265 922
O.S. Map: 195

ACCESS
Open. Park in the car park at SZ 264 925.

HABITAT
Crumbling undercliff.

STATUS
Unknown.

TARGET SPECIES
Glanville Fritillary (*Melitaea cinxia*).

TIMING
June week 1 to 3.

OTHER SPECIES
Common butterfly species occur plus migrants.

OTHER INFORMATION
This is the only mainland site for Glanville Fritillary where the species is considered to be naturally occuring.

Walk to the beach from the car park along the footpath then walk east to the undercliff.

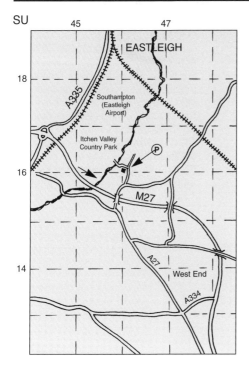

Grid Ref: SU 455 159
O.S. Map: 185 and 196

ACCESS
Open. Park near the country park visitor centre at SU 461 161.

HABITAT
Slow chalk stream adjacent to the River Itchen.

STATUS
Hampshire County Council Country Park.

TARGET SPECIES
Southern Damselfly (*Coenagrion mercuriale*).

TIMING
June week 4 to August week 2.

OTHER SPECIES
Hairy Dragonfly (*Brachytron pratense*) and Golden-ringed Dragonfly (*Corduligaster boltonii*), plus many common dragonfly species have been recorded. Silver-washed Fritillary *(Argynnis paphia)* and many common butterfly species are present.

OTHER INFORMATION
To find the Southern Damselfly walk behind the visitor centre, down a gravel track and over two gated bridges. Search the waterside vegetation either side of the second bridge. It is a first-class site for this species.

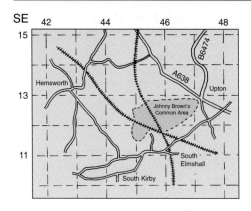

Grid Ref: SE 460 125
O.S. Map: 111

ACCESS
Site forms part of the Sesky Ringway footpath. Best access from disused railway line running towards South Kirkby from roundabout at junction of B6474/A638 near Upton. Best pond is down track on right. Other ponds take left fork of track. Many other access points from South Kirkby and South Elmsall.

HABITAT
Reclaimed colliery tips. Areas of marsh, meadow and young tree plantations. Area dotted with numerous small ponds.

STATUS
Site owned by Wakefield Metropolitan District Council. Managed for wildlife and as a green area for local community leisure activities. Parts of site have SSSI status for plant life.

TARGET SPECIES
Emperor Dragonfly (*Anax imperator*); Broad-bodied Chaser (*Libellula depressa*); Black-tailed Skimmer (*Orthetrum cancellatum*); Migrant Hawker (*Aeshna mixta*) and Ruddy Darter (*Sympetrum sanguineum*).

TIMING
June week 1 to July week 2 for Broad-bodied Chaser and Black-tailed Skimmer; June week 3 to July week 3 for Emperor Dragonfly; August weeks 2 to 4 for Ruddy Darter and Migrant Hawker.

OTHER SPECIES
At least 14 dragonfly and damselfly species recorded in 1997, including Azure, Common Blue, Blue-tailed and Emerald Damselflies and Four-spotted Chaser. Common Hawker, Brown Hawker, Common Darter and possible Black Darter occur.

OTHER INFORMATION
Best car park for disused railway line is lay-by 100 metres along B6474 towards South Elmsall.

Contact: John Wilcox, The South Elmsall, South Kirkby and Upton Area Environment Group, Broad Lane Business Centre, Westfield Lane, South Elmsall, West Yorkshire WF9 2JX. Tel: 01977 609939.

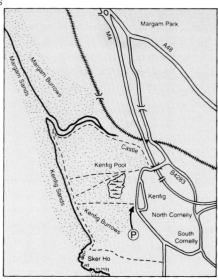

Grid Ref: SS 802 815
O.S. Map: 171

ACCESS
Public access. Park in reserve car park.

HABITAT
Dune slacks and ponds.

STATUS
National Nature Reserve and SSSI managed by Mid-Glamorgan County Council.

TARGET SPECIES
Keeled Skimmer (*Orthetrum coerulescens*); Ruddy Darter (*Sympetrum sanguineum*); Emperor Dragonfly (*Anax imperator*).

TIMING
A July visit should result in most target species being seen.

OTHER SPECIES
Over 20 species of dragonflies and damselflies have been recorded here including several Yellow-winged Darters in 1995.

OTHER FLORA AND FAUNA
Many plants typical of the different stages of dune formation can be found including Fen Orchid and Marsh Helleborine. The area is well known for its birdwatching, especially in the winter, but several species of wildfowl breed.

OTHER INFORMATION
A birdwatching hide is situated at the SW corner of Kenfig Pool. A leaflet on the dragonflies of the area is available from the Warden at the address below.

Contact: The Warden, Kenfig Nature Reserve Centre, Ton Kenfig, Pyle, Mid-Glamorgan CF33 4PT.

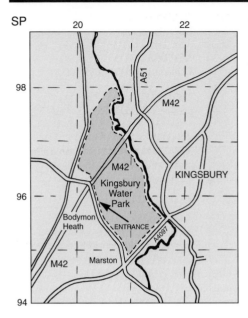

Grid Ref: SP 204 958 (entrance)
O.S. Map: 139

ACCESS
Off Bodymoor Heath Lane to the public car park (charge) and visitor centre.

HABITAT
Flooded gravel pits, scrub and grassland.

STATUS
Warwickshire County Council Reserve.

TARGET SPECIES
Red-eyed Damselfly (*Erythromma najas*); Emperor Dragonfly (*Anax imperator*); Black-tailed Skimmer (*Orthetrum cancellatum*); Migrant Hawker (*Aeshna mixta*).

TIMING
June week 2 to July week 4 for Red-eyed Damselfly, Emperor Dragonfly and Black-tailed Skimmer. August week 2 to September week 2 for Migrant Hawker.

OTHER SPECIES
Other common dragonfly and damselfly species occur. Many common butterflies are present and a small colony of Ringlet (*Aphantopus hyperantus*) has recently been found.

OTHER FLORA AND FAUNA
Many species of waterside and scrub-dwelling birds present.

OTHER INFORMATION
This large site has improved for dragonflies in the 1990's as species advance north. Contact: Kingsbury Water Park. Tel: 01827 872 660

> # ACCESS IS STRICTLY BY PERMIT ONLY.
>
> ## THE YORKSHIRE WILDLIFE TRUST WILL ISSUE DIRECTIONS TO THE SITE WITH THE PERMIT

ACCESS
Permit only.

HABITAT
Chalk grassland and scrub.

STATUS
Yorkshire Wildlife Trust Nature Reserve.

TARGET SPECIES
Dingy Skipper (*Erynnis tages*); Grayling (*Hipparchia semele*); Ringlet (*Aphantopus hyperantus*).

TIMING
May week 4 to June week 3 for Dingy Skipper, July week 2 to August week 1 for Grayling and Ringlet.

OTHER SPECIES
Many other common butterfly species have been recorded.

OTHER FLORA AND FAUNA
Amongst the plant species recorded are two of particular interest for the region, English Stonecrop and Adderstongue Fern.

OTHER INFORMATION
A permit must be obtained from the Yorkshire Wildlife Trust, 10 Toft Green, York YO1 1JT to visit this site.

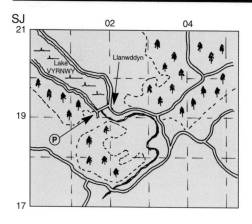

Grid Ref: SJ 016 190 (Information Centre and car park)
O.S. Map: 125

ACCESS
Public access. The Information Centre is most easily reached from the small town of Llanfyllin along the B4393 to Llanwddyn.

HABITAT
Broad-leaved and coniferous woodland, moorland.

STATUS
RSPB Nature Reserve.

TARGET SPECIES
Pearl-bordered Fritillary (*Boloria euphrosyne*); Small Pearl-bordered Fritillary (*Boloria selene*); Silver-washed Fritillary (*Argynnis paphia*); Purple Hairstreak (*Quercusia quercus*).

TIMING
May week 4 to June week 2 for Pearl-bordered Fritillary, June week 1 to July week 1 for Small Pearl-bordered Fritillary and July week 3 to August week 1 for Silver-washed Fritillary and Purple Hairstreak.

OTHER SPECIES
Ringlet (*Aphantopus hyperantus*) is amongst the numerous other butterfly species recorded.

OTHER FLORA AND FAUNA
The reserve supports a wide range of bird species including Red Grouse, Ring Ouzel, Buzzard, Pied Flycatcher, Redstart, Wood Warbler, Crossbill , Goosander and Grey Wagtail.

OTHER INFORMATION
A full day is needed to do justice to this excellent reserve. Time is best spent along the woodland trails. The moorland areas can be viewed from the Bala road.
Contact: Mike Walker, RSPB, Bryn Awel, Llanwyddn, Oswestry, Powys.

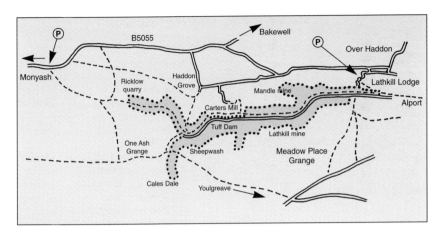

Grid Ref: SK 203 664 (car park at Over Haddon). SK157 665 (lay-by east of Monyash)
O.S. Map: 119

ACCESS
Public access, but keep to footpaths.

HABITAT
Limestone valley with woodland, cliffs, screes and grassland.

STATUS
National Nature Reserve.

TARGET SPECIES
Dingy Skipper (*Erynnis tages*); Northern Brown Argus (*Aricia artaxerxes*); Dark Green Fritillary (*Argynnis aglaja*).

TIMING
May week 4 to June week 2 for Dingy Skipper, June week 3 to July week 1 for Northern Brown Argus and July week 2 to August week 1 for Dark Green Fritillary.

OTHER SPECIES
A minimum of 19 species of butterfly have been noted.

OTHER FLORA AND FAUNA
The area has a wide range of limestone plants and a good population of birds. Slow Worm has been recorded.

OTHER INFORMATION
Doubt has recently occurred at this site regarding Northern Brown Argus, which some believe to be Brown Argus (*Aricia agestis*).

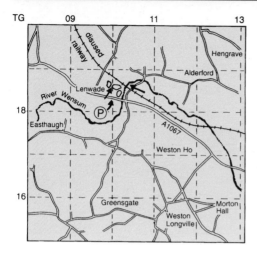

Grid Ref: TG 100 184 (parking)
O.S. Map: 133

ACCESS
Public access.

HABITAT
Large pools surrounded by scrub, restored meadows and mature trees. The River Wensum flows nearby.

TARGET SPECIES
Red-eyed Damselfly (*Erythromma najas*) on the lily pads on the lake at TG 101 186, Black-tailed Skimmer (*Orthetrum cancellatum*); Banded Demoiselle (*Calopteryx splendens*) where the old railway crosses the River Wensum.

TIMING
June week 2 to July week 3.

OTHER SPECIES
Many common species of damselfly and dragonfly are present.

OTHER FLORA AND FAUNA
A good range of common plant species plus a relatively rich birdlife.

OTHER INFORMATION
Red-eyed Damselfly is not particularly common in this region.

Duke of Burgundy — *A very scarce species in the North of England and declining in most of its range.*
(Colin Twist)

White-letter Hairstreak — *A very localised distribution, but probably under-recorded.* (Colin Twist)

Purple Emperor — *Photographed at Bentley Wood, Wiltshire in 1997. This is a classic site for this species.* (Colin Twist)

Fleetwith, Cumbria — *Home of one of the few English colonies of Mountain Ringlet.* (Colin Twist)

River Dee, Farndon in Cheshire — *One of only seven river systems where Club-tailed Dragonfly is found.* (Colin Twist)

Four-spotted Chaser — *The presence of this species often indicates rarer dragonflies may occur at the site.* (Colin Twist)

Ruddy Darter — *This dragonfly is extending its range into Northern England at a dramatic rate.*
(Colin Twist)

Club-tailed Dragonfly — *One of the rarest species and often found many kilometres away from the few river systems it occupies.*
(Colin Twist)

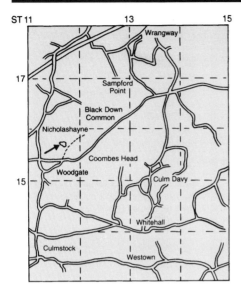

Grid Ref: ST 115 155
O.S. Map: 193

ACCESS
From Nicholashayne, follow the minor road south towards Woodgate. Turn left after about 400m at crossroads and up track. Park at Purchas Farm. Follow the bridleway north-east, turning east at the top of the hill.

HABITAT
The reserve is an area of heathy grassland on greensand, with Blackthorn and Birch.

STATUS
Butterfly Conservation Nature Reserve, SSSI.

TARGET SPECIES
Silver-washed Fritillary (*Argynnis paphia*); Pearl-bordered Fritillary (*Boloria euphrosyne*); Marbled White (*Melanargia galathea*).

TIMING
May week 3 to June week 2 for Pearl-bordered Fritillary, July week 1 to August week 2 for Silver-washed Fritillary and Marbled White.

OTHER SPECIES
Other common butterfly species are present.

OTHER FLORA AND FAUNA
Emperor Moth and Scarlet Tiger Moth.

OTHER INFORMATION
Other chalkhill butterfly species, such as Brown Argus (*Aricia agestis*) and Chalkhill Blue (*Lysandra coridon*) have been recorded.

Contact: Roger Sutton, 16 Ashford Road, Wellington, Somerset TA21 8QF.

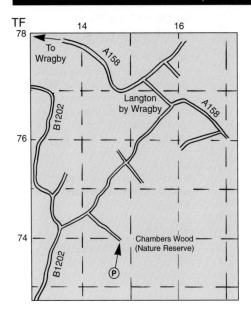

Grid Ref: TF 145 744
O.S. Map: 121

ACCESS
Park at Chambers Farm Wood,
signposted off the main roads.

HABITAT
Old grassland on heavy clay soil with
abundant meadow plants.

STATUS
Managed by Lincolnshire Trust for
Nature Conservation in agreement with
the Forestry Commission.

TARGET SPECIES
Grizzled Skipper (*Pyrgus malvae*); Dingy Skipper (*Erynnis tages*); White Admiral (*Ladoga camilla*) and Purple Hairstreak (*Quercusia quercus*).

TIMING
May week 2 to June week 1 for Grizzled Skipper, May week 4 to June week 3 for Dingy Skipper, all July for White Admiral and July week 3 to August week 2 for Purple Hairstreak.

OTHER SPECIES
Around 26 species of butterfly have been recorded on the reserve.

OTHER INFORMATION
For further information contact the Lincolnshire Trust for Nature Conservation, Banovallum House, Manor House Street, Horncastle, Lincolnshire LN9 5HF.

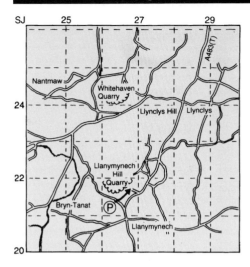

Grid Ref: SJ 266 218
O.S. Map: 126

ACCESS
Public access. Car parking is limited at the site, so please park carefully at SJ 267 217.

HABITAT
Disused quarry with spoil heaps.

STATUS
Nature reserve managed by the Shropshire and Montgomeryshire Wildlife Trusts.

TARGET SPECIES
Dingy Skipper (*Erynnis tages*); Grizzled Skipper (*Pyrgus malvae*).

TIMING
May week 2 to June week 1 for Grizzled Skipper, May week 4 to June week 3 for Dingy Skipper.

OTHER SPECIES
Pearl-bordered Fritillary (*Boloria euphrosyne*) and Small Pearl-bordered Fritillary (*Boloria selene*) have been recorded here.

OTHER FLORA AND FAUNA
Common Twayblade and Early Purple Orchid. Redstart nest in the quarry.

OTHER INFORMATION
Club-tailed Dragonfly were recorded here in 1995, 1996 and 1997.

A visit to the nearby Llynclys Common at SJ 273 237 later in the season may produce Ringlet (*Aphantopus hyperantus*) and Silver-washed Fritillary (*Argynnis paphia*).

Contact: Shropshire Wildlife Trust, Old St. George's School, New Street, Frankwell, Shrewsbury SY3 8JP.

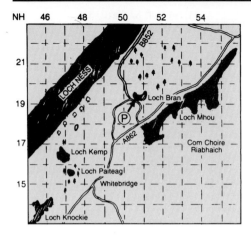

Grid Ref: NH 507 192 (parking)
O.S. Map: 34 and 35

ACCESS
Access along forest tracks to various lochans.
Loch Bran is at NH 507 192.

HABITAT
A complex of small, neutral to slightly alkaline lochans, bounded on the north-west by Loch Ness. The area is forested.

TARGET SPECIES
Brilliant Emerald (*Somatachlora metallica*).

TIMING
All July.

OTHER SPECIES
Ten species of dragonfly breed in the area, but none of the other Emerald dragonflies occur.

OTHER INFORMATION
Loch Bran is one of the favoured lochs in the complex, but they are all worth checking for Brilliant Emerald. The species has been recorded from at least 12 of the lochans to the north-east of Loch Kemp. It appears to favour lochans under 1 ha in extent in this area, but the same is not true for the other areas in Scotland where it occurs. Loch Kemp itself does not support Brilliant Emerald. Loch Paiteag has a good population.

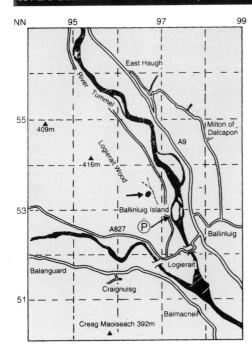

Grid Ref: NN 967 534
O.S. Map: 52

ACCESS
Open access. Park off the minor road sign-posted Hillhead Cemetery which runs north from Logierait. Follow the forest track to the pool.

HABITAT
Large forest with many conifers. The pool is surrounded by dense vegetation.

TARGET SPECIES
Northern Damselfly (*Coenagrion hastulatum*) at one of its classic sites.

TIMING
June week 4 to July week 3.

OTHER SPECIES
Common *Odonata* occur at this site.

OTHER INFORMATION
Identification problems occur as Common Blue is present in large numbers. Wellingtons are essential and care should be taken near the pool edges. A visit here could be combined with one to the Loch of the Lowes Scottish Wildlife Trust Reserve near Dunkeld. Ospreys have bred regularly here and give superb views. Ringlet (*Aphantopus hyperantus*) are also present. Grid Ref: NO 0544.

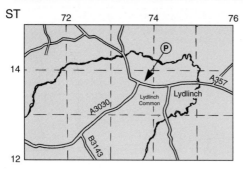

Grid Ref: ST 737 137 (lay-by parking area)
O.S. Map: 194

ACCESS
Open.

HABITAT
Grassland and scrub.

STATUS
SSSI.

TARGET SPECIES
Marsh Fritillary (*Eurodryas aurinia*); Dingy Skipper (*Erynnis tages*); Grizzled Skipper (*Pyrgus malvae*); Marbled White (*Melanargia galathea*); Silver-washed Fritillary (*Argynnis paphia*); Purple Hairstreak (*Quercusia quercus*).

TIMING
May week 4 to June week 2 for Marsh Fritillary, Dingy Skipper and Grizzled Skipper; July weeks 2 to 4 for Marbled White, Silver-washed Fritillary and Purple Hairstreak.

OTHER SPECIES
Brown Hairstdreak (*Thecla betulae*), Brown Argus (*Aricia agestis*) and White Admiral (*Ladoga camilla*) occur in small numbers. There is a good population of Ringlet (*Aphantopus hyperantus*).

OTHER FLORA AND FAUNA
Double figure pairs of Nightingales breed. Heath and Common Spotted Orchids occur plus a good range of interesting flowers.

OTHER INFORMATION
A pool has been re-excavated which may prove good for *Odonata*.

The areas both sides of the A357 should be explored from the lay-by.

Marsh Fritillary is also available nearby at Hod Hill (ST 857 107) but the site is very exposed.

Brown Hairstreak has been regularly recorded along public footpaths through Deadmoor Common (ST 752 111).

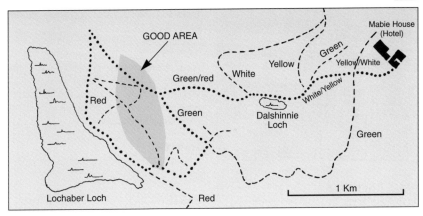

Grid Ref: NX 950 708 (parking at Mabie House)
O.S. Map: 84

ACCESS
Forest tracks are colour marked. Mabie House is 5 kilometres south of Dumfries just west of the A710.

HABITAT
Mainly Oak woodland.

STATUS
Forest Nature Reserve.

TARGET SPECIES
Small Pearl-bordered Fritillary (*Boloria selene*); Pearl-bordered Fritillary (*Boloria euphrosyne*); Dark Green Fritillary (*Argynnis aglaja*); Purple Hairstreak (*Quercusia quercus*).

TIMING
All June for Small Pearl-bordered Fritillary; May week 3 to June week 2 for Pearl-bordered Fritillary; July week 2 to August week 1 for Dark Green Fritillary and Purple Hairstreak.

OTHER SPECIES
Eighteen species recorded so far with a few more likely in the next few years. Needs exploring, but good for dragonflies.

OTHER FLORA AND FAUNA
Very good areas for Bluebells. A good population of Red Squirrel exists in the forest.

OTHER INFORMATION
A site visit could easily be combined with one of the RSPB reserves, i.e. Loch Ken, Mersehead or Wood of Cree. The coast around Kippford is worth exploring for Wall Brown and Grayling.

Contact: Mr S. Tamner, Forest Enterprise, AE Forest District, AE Village, Dumfries.

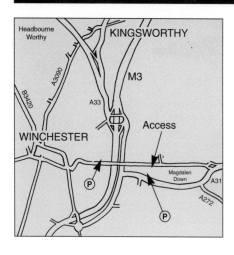

Grid Ref: SU 505 292
O.S. Map: 185

ACCESS
North entrance is immediately east of the Winchester Masonic Centre at SU 499 294. Park safely, well west of this point. South entrance is off Petersfield Road (A31) - park in the lay-by.

HABITAT
Regenerated south facing chalk downland, with some scrub.

STATUS
Butterfly Conservation Nature Reserve.

TARGET SPECIES
Brown Argus (*Aricia agestis*); Dingy Skipper (*Erynnis tages*); Marbled White (*Melanargia galathea*); Chalkhill Blue (*Lysandra coridon*).

TIMING
May week 4 to June week 3 for Brown Argus. August weeks 1 to 3 for Brown Argus (second brood) and Chalkhill Blue. June week 4 and all July for Marbled White.

OTHER SPECIES
Occasional sightings of Duke of Burgundy (*Hamearis lucina*) and Small Blue (*Cupido minimus*) have occurred.

OTHER FLORA AND FAUNA
Common Rock-rose, Ploughman's Spikenard, Chalk Milkwort, Clustered Bellflower.

OTHER INFORMATION
Dave Payne, 17 Millais Road, Woolston, Southampton SO19 2FY.

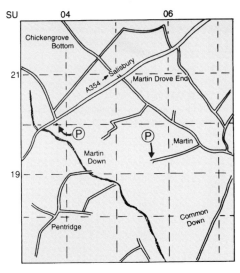

Grid Ref: SU 057 192 and SU 038 200 (parking)
O.S. Map: 184 / 195

ACCESS
Public access.

HABITAT
Chalk downland.

STATUS
National Nature Reserve, owned and managed by English Nature.

TARGET SPECIES
Adonis Blue (*Lysandra bellargus*); Chalkhill Blue (*Lysandra coridon*); Small Blue (*Cupido minimus*); Silver-spotted Skipper (*Hesperia comma*); Duke of Burgundy (*Hamearis lucina*); Marsh Fritillary (*Eurodryas aurinia*).

TIMING
May week 3 to June week 2 and August week 3 to September week 2 for Adonis Blue; July week 4 and all August for Chalkhill Blue; May week 4 to June week 2 for Small Blue and Duke of Burgundy; throughout June for Marsh Fritillary and August week 2 to September week 1 for Silver-spotted Skipper. Therefore a visit in either early June or late August would provide the best opportunity for most of the target species.

OTHER SPECIES
At least 43 species of butterfly have been recorded on the Reserve.

OTHER FLORA AND FAUNA
Horseshoe Vetch, Chalk Milkwort, Bastard Toadflax, Pasque Flower, Burnt-tipped, Frog, Man and Greater Butterfly Orchids. Nightingale, Nightjar, Hobby.

OTHER INFORMATION
A leaflet on the site is available from English Nature.

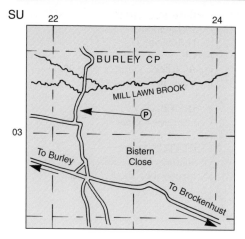

Grid Ref: SU 223 033 (car park)
O.S. Map: 195

ACCESS
Public access.

HABITAT
Open stream to vegetated/scrub stream with seepages, surrounded by lowland heath.

STATUS
The New Forest is Crown land managed by Forest Enterprise.

TARGET SPECIES
Scarce Blue-tailed Damselfly (*Ishnura pumilio*); Southern Damselfly (*Coenagrion mercuriale*); Small Red Damselfly (*Ceriargrion tenellum*).

TIMING
June week 4 to August week 1 for all species.

OTHER SPECIES
Keeled Skimmer (*Orthetrum coerulescens*), Beautiful Demoiselle (*Calopteryx virgo*). Black Darter (*Sympetrum danae*) and Common Hawker (*Aeshna juncea*) are also worth looking for in the general area.

OTHER INFORMATION
Walk east along the stream from the car park, checking the areas of seepage, especially where the stream divides.

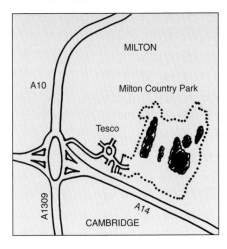

Grid Ref: TL 480 620
O.S. Map: 154

ACCESS
Public access. Car park open 08.00 am to dusk except Christmas Day.

HABITAT
Disused gravel pits.

STATUS
Country Park managed by South Cambridgeshire District Council.

TARGET SPECIES
Black-tailed Skimmer (*Orthetrum cancellatum*); Emperor Dragonfly (*Anax imperator*); Migrant Hawker (*Aeshna mixta*); Hairy Dragonfly (*Brachytron pratense*).

TIMING
May week 3 to June week 2 for Hairy Dragonfly, June week 2 to July week 2 for Black-tailed Skimmer and Emperor Dragonfly. August week 2 to September week 3 for Migrant Hawker.

OTHER SPECIES
At least eighteen species of *Odonata* have been recorded at the site with new species added as the site develops. Twenty-one butterfly species have also been recorded.

OTHER FLORA AND FAUNA
Hobby are seen at the country park most years. Muntjac Deer are present.

OTHER INFORMATION
A series of leaflets, including one on the dragonflies and one on the butterflies are available for 25p each from the Visitor Centre.

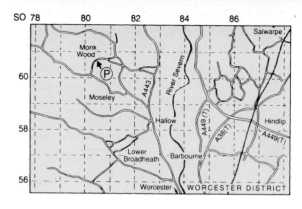

Grid Ref: SO 804 607 for parking and access
O.S. Map: 150

ACCESS
The reserve entrance is approx. 8kms north-west of Worcester.

HABITAT
Mixed broad-leaved plantation on an ancient woodland site.

STATUS
Butterfly Conservation and Worcestershire Wildlife Trust Nature Reserve.

TARGET SPECIES
Wood White (*Leptidea sinapis*); Dingy Skipper (*Erynnis tages*); Purple Hairstreak (*Quercusia quercus*); Silver-washed Fritillary (*Argynnis paphia*); White Admiral (*Ladoga camilla*).

TIMING
May week 4 to June week 3 for Wood White and Dingy Skipper. July for Silver-washed Fritillary and White Admiral. July week 4 to August week 3 for Purple Hairstreak.

OTHER SPECIES
Many common woodland species can be seen.

OTHER FLORA AND FAUNA
Over 500 species of moth have been recorded.

OTHER INFORMATION
Contact: Claire Turner, Simberton Bungalow, Monkwood Green, Hallow, Worcester WR2 6NX.

88

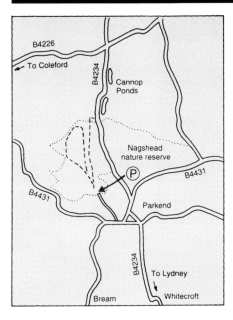

Grid Ref: SO 606 085 (car park)
O.S. Map: 162

ACCESS
Public access. Sign-posted off the B4431 at Parkend.

HABITAT
Mature broad-leaved woodland.

STATUS
RSPB Nature Reserve, SSSI. The site is leased by the RSPB from Forest Enterprise.

TARGET SPECIES
Silver-washed Fritillary (*Argynnis paphia*); Grizzled Skipper (*Pyrgus malvae*); Small Pearl-bordered Fritillary (*Boloria selene*); Beautiful Demoiselle (*Calopteryx virgo*).

TIMING
May week 2 to June week 1 for Grizzled Skipper, throughout June for Small Pearl-bordered Fritillary, throughout July for Silver-washed Fritillary, May week 4 to August week 1 for Beautiful Demoiselle.

OTHER SPECIES
Thirty-five species of butterfly and 21 dragonflies have been recorded on the reserve since 1974, though many are not recorded annually. Scarce Blue-tailed Damselfly have not been recorded since 1993.

OTHER FLORA AND FAUNA
Ivy-leaved Bellflower, Pied Flycatcher, Wood Warbler.

OTHER INFORMATION
The best places for seeing the various dragonflies and damselflies are around the pond near the information centre and from the hide overlooking the Lower Ponds.

Cannop Ponds has a large population of Mandarin Duck.

Contact: RSPB, The Puffins, Parkend, Lydney, Gloucestershire GL15 4JA.

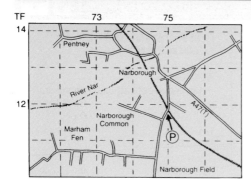

Grid Ref: TF 756 115
O.S. Map: 132

ACCESS
The reserve is just over 1km south of Narborough, on the minor road to Marham. Park at TF 750 118 (10 car spaces).

HABITAT
Disused railway line, with a rich grassland flora on chalk slopes of cuttings and embankments.

STATUS
Norfolk Wildlife Trust Reserve, managed by Butterfly Conservation.

TARGET SPECIES
Brown Argus (*Aricia agestis*); Dingy Skipper (*Erynnis tages*); Grizzled Skipper (*Pyrgus malvae*); Purple Hairstreak (*Quercusia quercus*); White-letter Hairstreak (*Strymonidia w-album*).

TIMING
May week 4 and June week 1 for Dingy and Grizzled Skippers and Brown Argus. July weeks 1 to 3 for White-letter Hairstreak. July week 4 to August week 3 for Purple Hairstreak and August weeks 2 to 4 for second brood Brown Argus.

OTHER SPECIES
Many common butterfly species can be seen, including abundant Brimstone (*Gonepteryx rhamni*).

OTHER FLORA AND FAUNA
Nightingale, Stripe-winged Grasshopper. Plants include Blue Fleabane, Ploughman's Spikenard, Stemless Thistle, Autumn Gentian, Thyme and Marjoram.

OTHER INFORMATION
Contact: Roland Rogers MBE, 1A Tuckswood Lane, Norwich, Norfolk NR4 6BD.

90

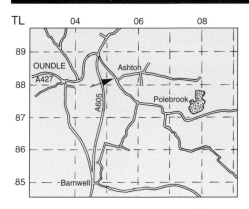

Grid Ref: TL 053 883
O.S. Map: 142

ACCESS
Open mid-June to late September; Saturdays, Sundays and Bank Holiday Monday 10.30 am to 5.00 pm.

HABITAT
2 acre wetland/lake, mill pond, mill race, surrounding scrub and grassland.

TARGET SPECIES
Emperor Dragonfly (*Anax imperator*); Ruddy Darter (*Sympetrum sanguineum*); Migrant Hawker (*Aeshna mixta*); Red-eyed Damselfly (*Erythromma najas*).

TIMING
June week 4 and all July for Emperor Dragonfly and Red-eyed Damselfly. All July and August for Ruddy Darter. August week 3 to September week 3 for Migrant Hawker

OTHER SPECIES
Sixteen species of dragonfly and damselfly have been recorded at the Museum.

OTHER INFORMATION
The Museum also contains exhibition areas, videos and live larvae in tanks. There are regular live larvae demonstrations using a TV microscope link. The museum has an extensive collection of adult and exuvia specimens and a very comprehensive library (collections and library by appointment only). Other attractions include a Victorian hydro-electric powerhouse, a fish collection, vintage farm machinery, a blacksmith's forge, tea room and gift shop.

A visit on the last two weekends of July and the middle two in August could be combined with the Ashton Water Dragonfly Sanctuary at TL 077 875, where a similar range of species can be encoutered.

Contact: National Dragonfly Museum, Ashton Wold, Ashton, Nr Oundle, Peterborough, PE8 5LZ. Tel: 01832 272427.

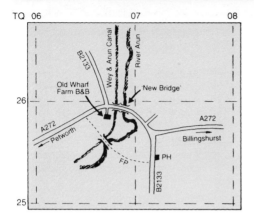

Grid Ref: TQ 068 260
O.S. Map: 197

ACCESS
Open access, but with difficult car parking. Park sensibly.

HABITAT
Disused canal and river.

TARGET SPECIES
White-legged Damselfly (*Platycnemis pennipes*); Hairy Dragonfly (*Brachytron pratense*); Downy Emerald (*Cordulia aenea*); Club-tailed Dragonfly (*Gomphus vulgatissimus*); Scarce Chaser (*Libellula fulva*).

TIMING
May week 4 to June week 2 for Club-tailed Dragonfly, Hairy Dragonfly, Downy Emerald and Scarce Chaser. June week 3 to July week 4 for White-legged Damselfly.

OTHER SPECIES
Sixteen species of dragonfly have been seen at the site.

OTHER INFORMATION
This site was first described in the BDS's Spring 1995 Newsletter by Ronnie Silsby, who we thank for allowing us to include the details.

Similar target species, with greater numbers of Club-tailed Dragonfly are available at Stopham Bridge where the A283 crosses the River Arun at TQ 030 184.

Nearby, Pulborough Brooks RSPB Reserve has commoner *Odonata*. It is sign-posted from the A283 between Pulborough and Storrington.

The Wildfowl and Wetlands Trust Reserve at Arundel is also worth a visit.

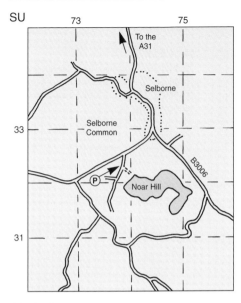

Grid Ref: SU 740 322 (reserve entrance)
O.S. Map: 186

ACCESS
Open. Park sensibly along the lane at SU 738 324.

HABITAT
Old chalkpits and scrub.

STATUS
Hampshire Wildlife Trust Reserve.

TARGET SPECIES
Duke of Burgundy (*Hamearis lucina*); Silver-washed Fritillary (*Argynnis paphia*); Brown Hairstreak (*Thecla betulae*).

TIMING
May week 3 to June week 1 for Duke of Burgundy; July weeks 2 to 4 for Silver-washed Fritillary; August week 3 to September week 1 for Brown Hairstreak.

OTHER SPECIES
Many common butterfly species are recorded.

OTHER FLORA AND FAUNA
A wide range of limestone plants including Musk Orchids are present. Nightingales are in good numbers.

OTHER INFORMATION
Considered by many to be the premier site for Brown Hairstreak which descends to Hemp Agrimony and other plants especially on the left side of the reserve. Collecting is expressly forbidden.

Donations following a visit would be gratefully received.

Avoid weekends in August whenever possible.

A visit to Gilbert White's house in nearby Selborne is of great interest.

Contact the Hampshire Wildlife Trust, 8 Romsey Road, Eastleigh, Hampshire SO50 9AL.

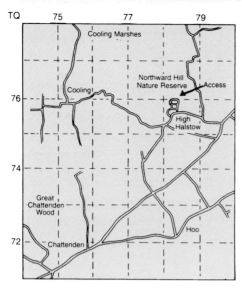

Grid Ref: TQ 784 764
O.S. Map: 178

ACCESS
Public access away from the heronry. Enter off Northward Avenue in High Halstow. Do not obstruct resident's driveways or access.

HABITAT
Oak woodland with Ash, Maple and Elm. Hawthorn thickets.

STATUS
RSPB Nature Reserve, SSSI, NNR.

TARGET SPECIES
White-letter Hairstreak (*Strymonidia w-album*); Purple Hairstreak (*Quercusia quercus*); Essex Skipper (*Thymelicus lineola*).

TIMING
July weeks 1 and 2 for White-letter Hairstreak, July week 3 to August week 2 for Purple Hairstreak, July week 3 to August week 2 for Essex Skipper.

OTHER SPECIES
Common woodland butterfly species occur.

OTHER FLORA AND FAUNA
The reserve contains Britain's largest heronry, all three woodpeckers, Nightingale and warblers.

OTHER INFORMATION
Possibly the best site in Britain for White-letter Hairstreak.

Contact: RSPB Northward Hill, Bromhey Farm, Eastborough, Cooling, Rochester, Kent ME3 8DS.

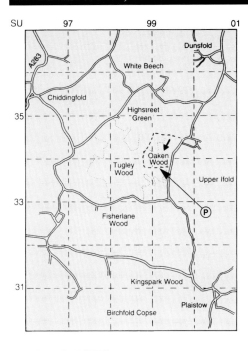

Grid Ref: SU 994 338 (parking)
O.S. Map: 186

ACCESS
Take the minor road between
Dunsfold and Plaistow, east of the
A283 Godalming-Petworth Road.
Limited car parking. Open access.

HABITAT
Woodland reserve with a mixture of
mature trees, coppice, scrub and
neutral grassland on clay.

STATUS
Butterfly Conservation Nature
Reserve.

TARGET SPECIES
Pearl-bordered Fritillary (*Boloria euphrosyne*); Small Pearl-bordered Fritillary (*Boloria selene*); Silver-washed Fritillary (*Argynnis paphia*); Wood White (*Leptidea sinapis*); Purple Emperor (*Apatura iris*); Brown Hairstreak (*Thecla betulae*); Grizzled Skipper (*Pyrgus malvae*).

TIMING
June week 1 and 2 for Pearl-bordered and Small Pearl-bordered Fritillary, Wood White and Grizzled Skipper; July weeks 2 and 3 for Silver-washed Fritillary and Purple Emperor; August weeks 2 to 4 for Brown Hairstreak.

OTHER SPECIES
Many other common woodland species - 35 species have bred on the site!

OTHER FLORA AND FAUNA
Wild Service Tree, Nightingale, Greater Butterfly Orchid. Moths include Large Red-belted and Yellow-legged Clearwings, Broad-bordered Bee Hawkmoth.

OTHER INFORMATION
The reserve is part of Forestry Enterprise managed woodland complex, which also includes Botany Bay. Explore all adjacent woodland where public rights of way exist.

Contact: Peter Beale, 7 Park Close, Alice Holt Lodge, Holt Pound, Farnham, Surrey. Peter would appreciate all records for the area.

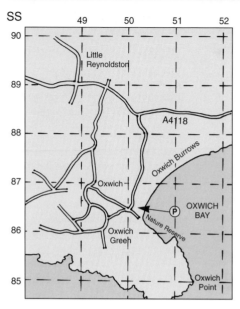

Grid Ref: SS 502 865 (parking)
O.S. Map: 159

ACCESS
Open access 10.00 am to noon weekends, 9.00 am to 1.00 pm weekdays. Charge for car park.

HABITAT
Sand-dune complex with fresh water and salt water marshes. Oak woodland.

STATUS
National Nature Reserve.

TARGET SPECIES
Dark Green Fritillary (*Argynnis aglaja*); Silver-washed Fritillary (*Argynnis paphia*); Purple Hairstreak (*Quercusia quercus*); White-letter Hairstreak (*Strymonidia w-album*).

TIMING
July weeks 2 to 4 for fritillaries, July weeks 1 to 3 for White-letter Hairstreak, July week 3 to August week 2 for Purple Hairstreak.

OTHER SPECIES
Over 20 species of butterfly are recorded most years including Dingy Skipper (*Erynnis tages*), Brimstone (*Gonepteryx rhamni*) and Grayling (*Hipparchia semele*).

OTHER FLORA AND FAUNA
The sand dunes are rich in wild flowers including Marsh Helleborine and Dune Gentian. The reedbeds offer good birdwatching and the marshes attract migrant waders and wildfowl.

OTHER INFORMATION
The reserve lies to the south-east of the village of Oxwich accessed off the A4118 Swansea to Port Eynon road.

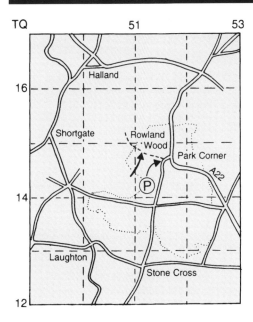

Grid Ref: TQ 511 148
O.S. Map: 199

ACCESS
The reserve is 2 km south of East Hoathly. Turn off the A22 at Park Corner and park in the lay-by on the right at TQ 515 147. Open access.

HABITAT
Broad-leaved woodland of Oak, Birch and Hornbeam with an area of heathy grassland.

STATUS
Butterfly Conservation Nature Reserve.

TARGET SPECIES
Small Pearl-bordered Fritillary (*Boloria selene*); Pearl-bordered Fritillary (*Boloria euphrosyne*); Silver-washed Fritillary (*Argynnis paphia*); Grizzled Skipper (*Pyrgus malvae*); White Admiral (*Ladoga camilla*).

TIMING
June weeks 1 and 2 for Grizzled Skipper, Pearl-bordered and Small Pearl-bordered Fritillaries; July weeks 2 to 4 for Silver-washed Fritillary and White Admiral.

OTHER SPECIES
Many common woodland and grassland butterflies occur.

OTHER FLORA AND FAUNA
Moths include Cream-spot Tiger, Broad-bordered Bee, Eyed, Elephant and Pine Hawkmoths. Dormouse. Good range of common dragonflies.

OTHER INFORMATION
Contact: Roger Carter, 31 Cuthbert Road, Brighton BN2 2EN.

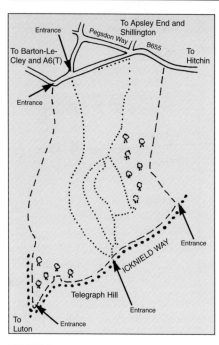

Grid Ref: TL 120 295
O.S. Map: 166

ACCESS
Take the B655 from Barton-le-Clay, through Hexton towards Hitchin. The reserve is located in the village of Pegsdon opposite the Live and Let Live Public House. Limited parking is available but do not obstruct resident's driveways or access.

HABITAT
Chalk grassland and associated species-rich scrub.

STATUS
Site of Special Scientific Interest and Wildlife Trust Nature Reserve.

TARGET SPECIES
Chalkhill Blue (*Lysandra coridon*); Brown Argus (*Aricia agestis*); Dingy Skipper (*Erynnis tages*).

TIMING
May week 4 to June week 1 for first brood Brown Argus and Dingy Skipper; August weeks 2 and 3 for second brood Brown Argus and Chalkhill Blue.

OTHER SPECIES
Many common species occur. Dark Green Fritillary (*Argynnis aglaja*) occasionally seen.

OTHER FLORA AND FAUNA
Chalk grassland specialists such as Horseshoe Vetch, Clustered Bellflower, Common Rock-rose and Wild Thyme. The site contains a healthy population of Glow-worms.

OTHER INFORMATION
Contact: Wildlife Trust, Priory Country Park, Barkers Lane, Bedford MK41 9SH.

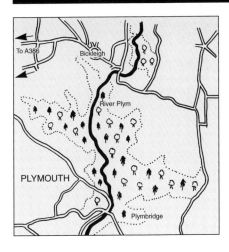

Grid Ref: SX 52 58
O.S. Map: 201

ACCESS
Open access

HABITAT
Mixed woodland with open glades.

STATUS
Owned by National Trust and Forest Enterprise.

TARGET SPECIES
Silver-washed Fritillary (*Argynnis paphia*); White Admiral (*Ladoga camilla*); Purple Hairstreak (*Quercusia quercus*).

TIMING
All July for White Admiral, July week 3 to August week 1 for Silver-washed Fritillary and Purple Hairstreak.

OTHER SPECIES
Thirty species of butterfly have been recorded in the woods.

OTHER FLORA AND FAUNA
The woods support many common bird species, plus Dipper along the River Plym.

OTHER INFORMATION
The area is on the northern outskirts of Plymouth and is well used by local residents at weekends, so mid-week visits may be best.

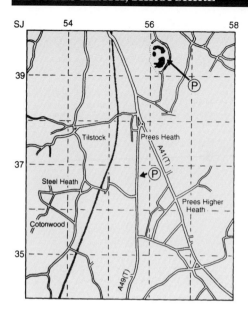

Grid Ref: SJ 558 368
O.S. Map: 126

ACCESS
Public access from the A49, south of Prees Heath village. Park carefully off the A49. Site immediately east of parking spot.

HABITAT
Rough heathland with scattered scrub.

STATUS
The site currently has no official status, but Butterfly Conservation launched an appeal to buy the site in 1995.

TARGET SPECIES
Silver-studded Blue (*Plebejus argus*) [in large numbers]; Small Skipper (*Thymelicus sylvestris*).

TIMING
July weeks 1 to 4.

OTHER SPECIES
Many other common butterflies occur.

OTHER INFORMATION
A visit here can be combined with Whixall Moss or with Brown Moss at SJ 564 394. The latter is an old peat bog which has reverted to a dry acid heath, woodland and pools. Dragonflies include Broad-bodied Chaser (*Libellula depressa*).

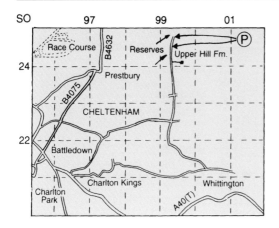

Grid Ref: SO 992 242 (southern half), SO 992 248 (northern half)
O.S. Map: 163

ACCESS
Park at either SO 993 244 or SO 994 247. Open access.

HABITAT
Limestone and neutral grassland, with small areas of heath.

STATUS
Butterfly Conservation Nature Reserve.

TARGET SPECIES
Duke of Burgundy (*Hamearis lucina*); Brown Argus (*Aricia agestis*); Chalkhill Blue (*Lysandra coridon*); Small Blue (*Cupido minimus*); Dark Green Fritillary (*Argynnis aglaja*); Marbled White (*Melanargia galathea*); Grayling (*Hipparchia semele*).

TIMING
May week 3 to June week 2 for Duke of Burgundy, Brown Argus and Small Blue; July week 2 to August week 1 for Dark Green Fritillary, Marbled White and Grayling. August for Chalkhill Blue and second brood Brown Argus.

OTHER INFORMATION
The two areas of limestone grassland making up the reserve are high on the Cotswold scarp slope to the north-east of Cheltenham and afford excellent views across the Severn Valley and beyond. Overlying the Oolitic limestone are thin deposits of ancient windblown sands, the combination of which gives rise to the very rich mix of limestone and neutral grassland flora. The two halves of the reserve are separated by a Beech plantation.

Contact: Simon Glover, Brook Cottage, Two Bridges, Blakeney, Gloucestershire GL15 4AF.

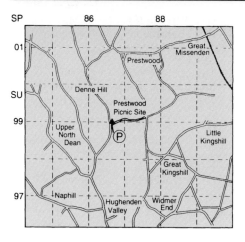

Grid Ref: SU 866 991
O.S. Map: 165

ACCESS
Open access.

HABITAT
Rough chalk grassland and scrub on a steep west-facing slope.

STATUS
Local Nature Reserve managed by Butterfly Conservation.

TARGET SPECIES
Dingy Skipper (*Erynnis tages*); Essex Skipper (*Thymelicus lineola*); Grizzled Skipper (*Pyrgus malvae*); Marbled White (*Melanargia galathea*); Dark Green Fritillary (*Argynnis aglaja*).

TIMING
May week 4 to June week 1 for Dingy and Grizzled Skippers, July weeks 2 to 4 for Essex Skipper, Marbled White and Dark Green Fritillary.

OTHER FLORA AND FAUNA
Silver Hook Moth, Clustered Bellflower, Autumn Gentian, Bee Orchid. Glow-worm and Orange Ladybird are resident.

OTHER INFORMATION
The site is opened at dawn and closed at dusk daily. Owing to part of the site once being a scrap yard it escaped much of the surrounding development and was purchased by the local council in 1970's. Conservation work carried out by BBCS has resulted in the site becoming a Local Nature Reserve.

Contact: Ron Beaven, 7 Chestnut Avenue, High Wycombe, Buckinghamshire.

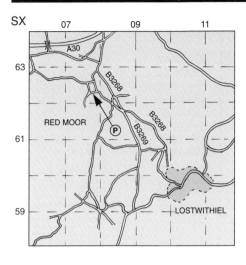

Grid Ref: SX 076 623 (parking)
O.S. Map: 200

ACCESS
The reserve entrance is 100 metres from the parking area, on the right down the track south to Creney Farm.

HABITAT
Scrub, heath, bog and ponds.

STATUS
Cornwall Wildlife Trust Reserve. SSSI.

TARGET SPECIES
Marsh Fritillary (*Eurodryas aurinia*); Silver-studded Blue (*Plebejus argus*); Small Red Damselfly (*Ceriagrion tenellum*).

TIMING
May week 4 to June week 2 for Marsh Fritillary; July week 2 to August week 1 for Silver-studded Blue; all July for Small Red Damselfly.

OTHER SPECIES
Sixteen species of *Odonata* have been recorded.

OTHER FLORA AND FAUNA
An interesting range of plants including Royal Fern and Round-leaved Sundew plus Adder and Grass Snake on the heath.

OTHER INFORMATION
Contact: Cornwall Wildlife Trust, Five Acres, Allet, Truro TR4 9DJ.

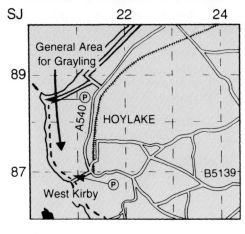

Grid Ref: SJ 205 875 (general area)
O.S. Map: 108

ACCESS
Open access along the beach. Do not enter fenced off areas or golf course. Park at Red Rocks in Hoylake or at West Kirby.

HABITAT
Dune system, reedmarsh and grassland.

STATUS
SSSI, Cheshire Wildlife Trust Nature Reserve.

TARGET SPECIES
Grayling (*Hipparchia semele*).

TIMING
July week 3 to August week 3.

OTHER SPECIES
Many common butterfly species. The site is well-positioned to attract migrant butterflies and moths.

OTHER FLORA AND FAUNA
Typical duneland flora can be seen. Migrant passerines in spring and autumn. Natterjack Toad.

OTHER INFORMATION
Please keep to the footpaths and boardwalks on this site, and do not allow dogs to enter the fenced area. Regular ringing takes place at the site during the migration periods.

A visit here can be combined with one to the Wirral Way.

Contact: Cheshire Wildlife Trust, Grebe House, Reaseheath, Nantwich, Cheshire CW5 6DA.

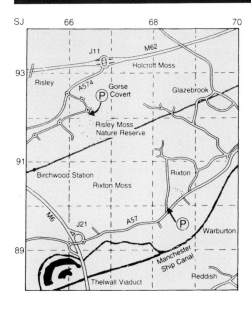

Grid Ref: RISLEY - SJ 664 921;
RIXTON - SJ 684 900
O.S. Map: 109

ACCESS
Risley open Saturday to Thursday
10am to 5pm. Keep to marked
footpaths. Rixton open at all times.

HABITAT
Risley is a remnant raised bog with
large wooded areas. Rixton is a
naturally reclaimed site with a variety
of habitats including clay pits.

STATUS
Both sites are SSSI's and managed by
the appropriate Ranger Services.

TARGET SPECIES
Common Hawker (*Aeshna juncea*) and Black Darter (*Sympetrum danae*) at both sites.

TIMING
All August.

OTHER SPECIES
Nine common species of *Odonata*, plus the two target species breed at both sites. Many
common butterflies, including Small Skipper (*Thymelicus sylvestris*) at Rixton.

OTHER FLORA AND FAUNA
Common woodland birds occur at both sites.

OTHER INFORMATION
Risley Moss was used as a munitions testing area, so there is no public access to the
mossland, but the target species can be seen from the many footpaths.

More freedom of movement available at Rixton.

Contact: Risley Moss - Cheshire County Council Countryside Management Service, Risley
Moss, Ordnance Way, Birchwood, Nr Warrington, Cheshire WA3 6QX.
Rixton Claypits - Warrington Ranger Service, Town Hall, West Annexe, Warrington
Cheshire.

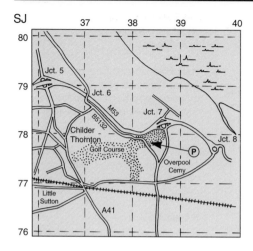

Grid Ref: SJ 384 778 (car park)
O.S. Map: 117

ACCESS
Public Access

HABITAT
Woodland, scrub and grassland.

STATUS
Local Nature Reserve managed by
Ellesmere Port and Neston Borough
Council.

TARGET SPECIES
Purple Hairstreak (*Quercusia quercus*); White-letter Hairstreak (*Strymonidia w-album*);
Small Skipper (*Thymelicus sylvestris*); Emperor Dragonfly (*Anax imperator*); Broad-
bodied Chaser (*Libellula depressa*); Ruddy Darter (*Sympetrum sanguineum*).

TIMING
June for Broad-bodied Chaser, July weeks 1 to 3 for White-letter Hairstreak, Small Skipper
and Emperor Dragonfly. July week 3 to August week 3 for Purple Hairstreak and Ruddy
Darter. Timing for Broad-bodied Chaser and Emperor Dragonfly can be beyond the stated
periods.

OTHER SPECIES
Common butterfly, dragonfly and damselfly species are present. Yellow-winged Darter
(*Sympetrum flaveolem*) was recorded in 1995. Banded Demoiselle (*Calopteryx splendens*)
has been recorded by the stream.

OTHER FLORA AND FAUNA
A good cross-section of woodland birds are present.

OTHER INFORMATION
The small pool near the ranger cabin by the car park has regular Broad-bodied Chaser. The
path by the stream either side of the B5132 has Wych Elm for the White-letter Hairstreaks.
Ponds in and adjacent to the Local Nature Reserve have Emperor Dragonfly and Ruddy
Darter.

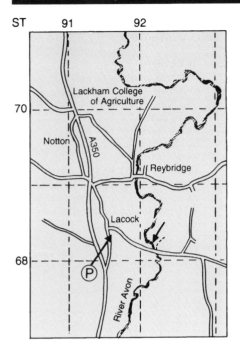

Grid Ref: ST 922 682
O.S. Map: 163

ACCESS
Public footpath along the river. Park in National Trust car park. Access to various ornamental ponds in the Abbey is by ticket from National Trust gatehouse.

HABITAT
Well vegetated river bank and ornamental ponds.

STATUS
National Trust property.

TARGET SPECIES
White-legged Damselfly (*Platycnemis pennipes*) along the River Avon.

TIMING
June week 2 to August week 1.

OTHER SPECIES
Many common species of dragonfly and damselfly occur around the ornamental ponds.

OTHER FLORA AND FAUNA
Typical woodland and farmland species of birds can be seen. Grey Wagtail occur along the stream.

OTHER INFORMATION
Lacock village is owned and managed by the National Trust, and is worth a visit for its historical interest. It also provides a useful 'breaking point' for journeys south just off the M4.

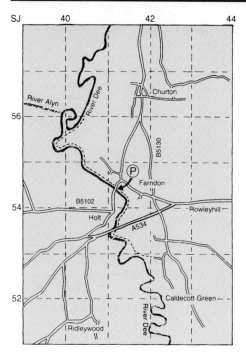

Grid Ref: SJ 413 545
O.S. Map: 117

ACCESS
Public access along the east side of the river north and south of Farndon.

HABITAT
Rather uninspired bank vegetation, with farmland flanking the river.

TARGET SPECIES
Club-tailed Dragonfly (*Gomphus vulgatissimus*) at the extreme north of its range. Banded Demoiselle (*Calopteryx splendens*).

TIMING
May week 4 to June week 2.

OTHER SPECIES
Some common damselflies occur.

OTHER FLORA AND FAUNA
As the river flows through agricultural land, there is little other wildlife.

OTHER INFORMATION
It may be necessary to walk up to 1 km south of Farndon and 2 km north. Be prepared to spend a full day without a firm guarantee of seeing Club-tailed Dragonfly. The classic site in England for Club-tailed Dragonfly is on the River Thames south of Goring where the railway line crosses the river. O.S. Map: 175. SU 609 795.

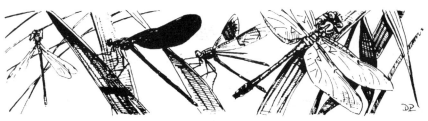

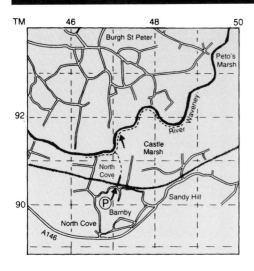

Grid Ref: TM 473 917 (River Waveney)

O.S. Map: 134

ACCESS
Public access to River Waveney. Permit required for Castle Marshes, contact Suffolk Wildlife Trust. Parking for River Waveney TM 471 904.

HABITAT
River Waveney is a well vegetated river. Castle Marshes are improved grazing marshes interlaced with ditches.

STATUS
Castle Marshes; SSSI, Suffolk Wildlife Trust Nature Reserve.

TARGET SPECIES
Scarce Chaser (*Libellula fulva*) along the River Waveney. Norfolk Hawker (*Aeshna isosceles*) and Hairy Dragonfly (*Brachytron pratense*) at Castle Marshes.

TIMING
June week 2 to 4 for Norfolk Hawker and Scarce Chaser; May week 4 to June week 2 for Hairy Dragonfly.

OTHER SPECIES
Some other common species of dragonfly occur.

OTHER INFORMATION
North Cove Suffolk Wildlife Trust Reserve is at TM 471 906 just north-west of the railway crossing. It is well worth checking for *Odonata* when visiting the area.

For a permit for Castle Marshes, contact Suffolk Wildlife Trust, Brooke House, The Green, Ashboching, Ipswich IP6 9JY.

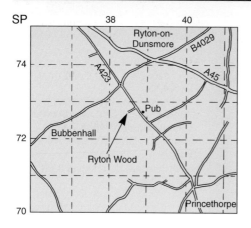

Grid Ref: SP 387 728 (entrance off the A423)
O.S. Map: 140

ACCESS
Permit only.

HABITAT
Mixed woodland with a large amount of Oak and a rich understorey.

STATUS
Warwickshire Wildlife Trust Nature Reserve. SSSI.

TARGET SPECIES
White Admiral (*Ladoga camilla*); Purple Hairstreak (*Quercusia quercus*); Marbled White (*Melanargia galathea*); Small Pearl-bordered Fritillary (*Boloria selene*) (introduced on a recovery scheme); White-letter Hairstreak (*Strymonidia w-album*).

TIMING
June weeks 2 to 4 for Small Pearl-bordered Fritillary, July weeks 2 to 4 for White Admiral, all July for Marbled White, July weeks 1 to 3 for White-letter Hairstreak and July week 3 to August week 2 for Purple Hairstreak.

OTHER SPECIES
Silver-washed Fritillary (*Argynnis paphia*) and Brown Argus (*Aricia agestis*) are recorded in small numbers. Over 30 species of butterfly and common *Odonata* in good numbers, have been recorded, the latter around the pool areas.

OTHER FLORA AND FAUNA
Woodland birds including Nightingale are present. Grass Snake and Muntjac Deer. Since 1990, 576 moths including 43 nationally important species have been noted.

OTHER INFORMATION
Permit from Warwickshire Wildlife Trust, Brandon Marsh Nature Centre, Brandon Lane, Coventry CV3 3GW. A visit will take a minimum of 2 hours.

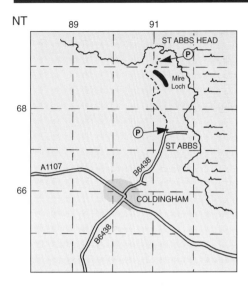

Grid Ref: NT 91 69 (general area)
O.S. Map: 67

ACCESS
Open. Parking at NT 912 692 or NT
913 674.

HABITAT
Sea cliffs, grassland and scrub.

STATUS
National Nature Reserve and SSSI.

TARGET SPECIES
Northern Brown Argus (*Aricia artaxerxes*); Ringlet (*Aphantopus hyperantus*); Dark Green
Fritillary (*Argynnis aglaja*); Grayling (*Hipparchia semele*).

TIMING
June week 2 to July week 2 for Northern Brown Argus; July weeks 2 to 4 for Ringlet,
Dark Green Fritillary and Grayling.

OTHER SPECIES
Many common butterflies occur.

OTHER FLORA AND FAUNA
Extensive seabird nesting colonies on the cliffs. Good clifftop flora and productive for
moths, including migrants.

OTHER INFORMATION
Northern Brown Argus can be found by the loch near the overflow dam and above the
divers car park at Pettico Wick.

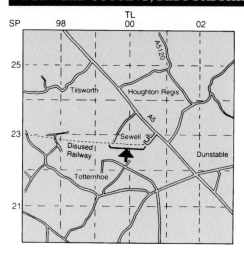

Grid Ref: SP 995 227 to TL 004 227
O.S. Map: 165 and 166

ACCESS
Public access.

HABITAT
Old railway cutting in chalk.

STATUS
Reserve managed by South
Bedfordshire District Council.

TARGET SPECIES
Small Blue (*Cupido minimus*).

TIMING
May week 4 to June week 2.

OTHER SPECIES
Marbled White (*Melanargia galathea*), Chalkhill Blue (*Lysandra coridon*) and Brown
Argus (*Aricia agestis*) may also occur later in the season.

OTHER FLORA AND FAUNA
Good examples of typical chalkland flora are present.

OTHER INFORMATION
A premier site, near the M1 just west of Dunstable, for Small Blue.

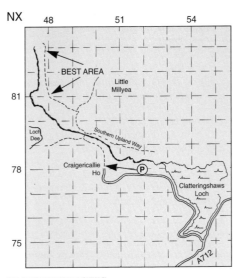

Grid Ref: NX 480810 to NX 478 830 along track.

O.S. Map: 77

ACCESS
Open along the forest tracks. Do not go on to the bog itself. Park at the road end along the west side of Clatteringshaws Loch at NX 503 781 at Craigencallie. Walk the forest tracks to the target area.

HABITAT
The Flowe itself is blanket bog. The forest tracks are through woodland with a large amount of conifer.

STATUS
The Flowe is a NNR.

TARGET SPECIES
Azure Hawker (*Aeshna caerulea*); Golden-ringed Dragonfly (*Cordulegaster boltonii*); Common Hawker (*Aeshna juncea*); Large Heath (*Coenonympha tullia*); Small Pearl-bordered Fritillary (*Boloria selene*); Scotch Argus (*Erebia aethiops*).

TIMING
July weeks 1 to 3 for all but Scotch Argus, which flies July week 4 to August week 2.

OTHER SPECIES
Other common *Odonata* and butterfly species occur.

OTHER FLORA AND FAUNA
Common Buzzard and other typical birds of the area and habitat can be encountered. Red Deer are common.

OTHER INFORMATION
The Azure Hawker perches on boulders and is best sought along the forest track between the above references along with the other dragonfly species. The butterflies are found along the forest tracks. Strong footwear is required although the walking is not arduous. Good, sunny weather is essential. This is the only Azure Hawker site south of the Highlands and possibly the best of all.

Grid Ref: SX 829 442 & SX 823 424 (car parks)
O.S. Map: 202

ACCESS
Open access, with permit from Field Centre required for some areas.

HABITAT
Freshwater lagoon with reedbeds and encroaching scrub.

STATUS
Managed by the Field Study Centre on behalf of the owners.

TARGET SPECIES
Migrant Hawker (*Aeshna mixta*); Hairy Dragonfly (*Brachytron pratense*); Downy Emerald (*Cordulea aenea*); Southern Damselfly (*Coenagrion mercuriale*).

TIMING
May week 4 to June week 2 for Hairy Dragonfly, May week 4 to July week 1 for Downy Emerald, June week 4 to August week 1 for Southern Damselfly, August week 2 to September week 3 for Migrant Hawker.

OTHER SPECIES
At least 17 species of dragonfly and damselfly have been recorded at Slapton Ley.

OTHER FLORA AND FAUNA
The area is botanically rich – it is the only known British site for Strapwort. The area is well known for birdwatching at all times of the year, especially during the migration periods and in winter.

OTHER INFORMATION
Devon Birdwatching and Preservation Society have a ringing station on the site. Contact: Slapton Ley Field Studies Centre, Slapton, Devon.

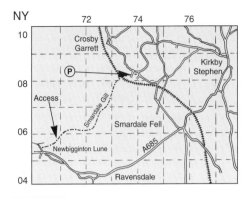

Grid Ref: NY 739 083 (car park at north end)
O.S. Map: 91

ACCESS
Northern car park in Smardale where the road goes under the disused railway line. Southern access is by parking in Newbiggin-on-Lune, walking towards Friar Bottom Farm from where a public footpath joins the reserve at NY 708 058. Open access.

HABITAT
Disused railway line over 5 kms long.

STATUS
Cumbria Wildlife Trust Reserve. SSSI.

TARGET SPECIES
Dingy Skipper (*Erynnis tages*); Northern Brown Argus (*Aricia artaxerxes*); Dark Green Fritillary (*Argynnis aglaja*); Scotch Argus (*Erebia aethiops*).

TIMING
June weeks 1 to 3 for Dingy Skipper, June week 3 to July week 2 for Northern Brown Argus, July for Dark Green Fritillary and July week 4 to August week 2 for Scotch Argus.

OTHER SPECIES
Common species typical of the habitat occur.

OTHER FLORA AND FAUNA
Redstart, Wood Warbler, Pied Flycatcher and Common Buzzard are notable. Roe Deer and Red Squirrel occur. Dipper by the viaduct.

OTHER INFORMATION
Visitors are encouraged to send a donation to the Cumbria Wildlife Trust if not already members. This reserve along with Arnside Knott, hold the only English colonies of Scotch Argus.

Contact: Cumbria Wildlife Trust, Brockhole, Windermere, Cumbria, LA23 1LJ

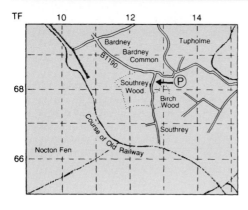

Grid Ref: TF 127 682
O.S. Map: 121

ACCESS
The reserve lies between Bardney and Southrey on B1190. Access is along the various forest rides.

HABITAT
A clear-felled area of woodland, which is naturally regenerating with native broad-leaves. The whole site is managed by Forest Enterprise as commercial woodland.

STATUS
Butterfly Conservation Nature Reserve. Woodland managed by Forest Enterprise.

TARGET SPECIES
White Admiral (*Ladoga camilla*); Purple Hairstreak (*Quercusia quercus*); Brown Hairstreak (*Thecla betulae*).

TIMING
July for White Admiral, July week 3 to August week 2 for Purple Hairstreak and August weeks 3 and 4 for Brown Hairstreak.

OTHER SPECIES
Many common butterflies occur on the site.

OTHER FLORA AND FAUNA
Yellow Archangel, Devilsbit Scabious, Early Purple Orchid. Birds include Woodcock and Nightingale. Grass Snakes are present.

OTHER INFORMATION
Other woodlands in the area are also of interest, including the Chambers Wood Forest Nature Reserve. Most are FE owned and open to the public along forest rides.

Contact: Peter Cawdell, Lowthorpe, Southrey, Lincoln LN3 5TD.

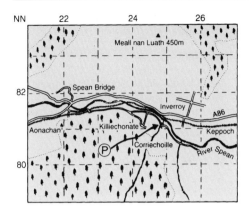

Grid Ref: NN 248 811
O.S. Map: 41

ACCESS
Open access. Explore the areas either side of the river to the south and by the road.

HABITAT
Rough grassland with scattered scrub and boggy areas.

TARGET SPECIES
Chequered Skipper (*Carterocephalus palaemon*); Small Pearl-bordered Fritillary (*Boloria selene*).

TIMING
May week 4 to June week 2.

OTHER SPECIES
Golden-ringed Dragonfly (*Cordulegaster boltonii*) is present plus common damselfly species.

OTHER FLORA AND FAUNA
Globeflower and Wood Cranesbill grow on the site. The moths here are worthy of study.

OTHER INFORMATION
Sunny days are essential for the target species.

If unsuccessful here for Chequered Skipper try the road along Loch Arkaig where the forestry plantations meet the road.

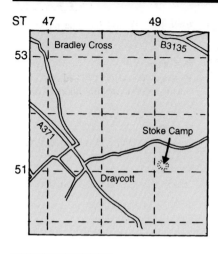

Grid Ref: ST 492 512
O.S. Map: 182

ACCESS
In Draycott village along the A371, turn uphill by the old Methodist Chapel (now flats) and proceed for over 1km. Park by the entrance for the Somerset WT reserve and cross the road into the field opposite. The reserve entrance is in the far wall.

HABITAT
Steeply sloping limestone grassland.

STATUS
Butterfly Conservation Nature Reserve.

TARGET SPECIES
Chalkhill Blue (*Lysandra coridon*); Small Blue (*Cupido minimus*); Brown Argus (*Aricia agestis*); Marbled White (*Melanargia galathea*); Dark Green Fritillary (*Argynnis aglaja*).

TIMING
May week 4 to June week 1 for Small Blue and Brown Argus; August for 2nd brood Brown Argus and Chalkhill Blue; July for Marbled White and Dark Green Fritillary.

OTHER SPECIES
Grayling (*Hipparchia semele*).

OTHER FLORA AND FAUNA
Green-winged Orchid, Autumn Lady's Tresses and Horseshoe Vetch.

OTHER INFORMATION
The nearby Somerset Wildlife Trust Reserve is *very* worth a look.

Contact: Hamish Cole, No. 2 The Manor Cottages, Stoke Street, Rodney Stoke, Cheddar BS27 3UN.

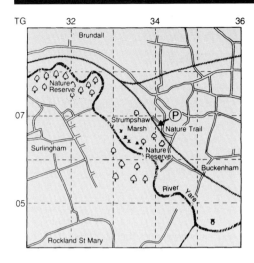

Grid Ref: TG 341 067 (car park)
O.S. Map: 134

ACCESS
Public access along marked paths during reserve opening hours from 9 a.m.

HABITAT
Open mixed fen and grazing marshes.

STATUS
RSPB Nature Reserve, SSSI.

TARGET SPECIES
Swallowtail (*Papilio machaon*); Norfolk Hawker (*Aeshna isoceles*); Black-tailed Skimmer (*Orthetrum cancellatum*); Migrant Hawker (*Aeshna mixta*).

TIMING
June weeks 2 and 3 for Swallowtail and Norfolk Hawker, June and July for Black-tailed Skimmer, August week 2 to September week 2 for Migrant Hawker.

OTHER SPECIES
Many common butterflies and dragonflies are present. Scarce Chaser (*Libellula fulva*) has been noted.

OTHER FLORA AND FAUNA
Marsh Harrier, Bearded Tit, Cetti's Warbler. Over 400 species of plants have been recorded including Water Soldier, Marsh Sow-thistle, Great Spearwort and Marsh Pea. Chinese Water Deer may be encountered.

OTHER INFORMATION
A visit to this site could be combined with one to any of the other Broadland sites, such as Upton Fen and River Waveney. Another fine site for Swallowtail is Hickling Broad Norfolk Wildlife Trust Nature Reserve accessed at TG 427 221. Charge for non-members.

Contact: RSPB, Staithe Cottage, Low Road, Strumpshaw, Norwich NR13 4HS.

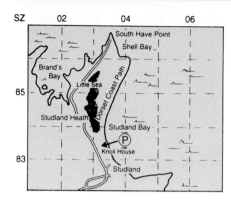

Grid Ref: SZ 035 835
O.S. Map: 195

ACCESS
Public access. Park in National Trust car park at Park Knoll SZ 031 835, or in one of the parking bays along the toll road to observe Poole Harbour.

HABITAT
Heathland, mixed woodland, ponds and wet areas.

STATUS
National Nature Reserve, SSSI, partially owned and managed by National Trust.

TARGET SPECIES
White Admiral (*Ladoga camilla*); Silver-studded Blue (*Plebejus argus*); Grayling (*Hipparchia semele*); Ruddy Darter (*Sympetrum sanguineum*).

TIMING
July.

OTHER SPECIES
Many common butterfly and dragonfly species can be seen.

OTHER FLORA AND FAUNA
Dartford Warbler, Hobby. Growing numbers of Little Egret can be seen roosting on Little Sea within the heath or feeding out in Poole Harbour. They have bred nearby.

Every species of British reptile present but almost impossible to see.

The area is very rich in grasshoppers and crickets.

OTHER INFORMATION
There is a visitor centre and cafe at the National Trust car park. A visit can be combined with a day on the beach, which can get very busy during the school holiday periods.

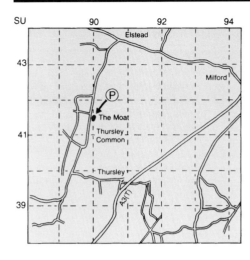

Grid Ref: SU 900 417 (Car Park)
O.S. Map: 186

ACCESS
Open access, though visitors must keep to the footpaths.

HABITAT
A large area of heath, bog and woodland.

STATUS
National Nature Reserve managed by English Nature.

TARGET SPECIES
Downy Emerald (*Cordulia aenea*); Keeled Skimmer (*Orthetrum coerulescens*); Small Red Damselfly (*Ceriagrion tenellum*); Brilliant Emerald (*Somatachlora metallica*).

TIMING
July weeks 1 and 2 are generally the best for the target species.

OTHER SPECIES
Twenty-six species have bred. Emperor Dragonfly (*Anax imperator*) and Broad-bodied Chaser (*Libellula depressa*) are present. Butterflies include Silver-studded Blue (*Plebejus argus*) and Grayling (*Hipparchia semele*). White-faced Darter is now considered extinct here.

OTHER FLORA AND FAUNA
Sixty-nine species of bird regularly breed on the reserve and the wet heaths and boggy areas have an interesting flora.

OTHER INFORMATION
This is a major location in Britain for dragonflies and worthy of a full day visit. Could possibly be combined with Oaken Wood.

Brilliant Emerald can be difficult here in some years.

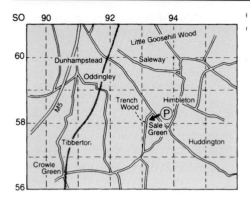

Grid Ref: SO 925 587
O.S. Map: 150

ACCESS
North of Sale Green village. The north-west and south-west corners of the wood are privately owned with no public access. The remainder of the wood is open to the public. Park at Sole Green at SO 932 582.

HABITAT
An ancient woodland clear-felled in the 1940's and replanted with Hazel, Silver Birch, Grey Alder and Sycamore.

STATUS
Butterfly Conservation and Worcestershire Wildlife Trust Nature Reserve.

TARGET SPECIES
White Admiral (*Ladoga camilla*); White-letter Hairstreak (*Strymonidia w-album*).

TIMING
July weeks 1 and 2.

OTHER SPECIES
Occasional Brown Argus (*Aricia agestis*) and Grizzled Skipper (*Pyrgus malvae*).

OTHER FLORA AND FAUNA
Herb Paris, Adderstongue Fern, Common Twayblade, Meadow Saffron.

OTHER INFORMATION
Contact: Ken Thomas, 34 Froxmere Close, Crowle, Worcester WR7 4AP.

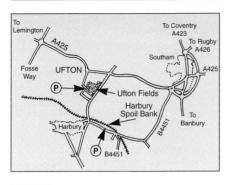

Grid Ref: SP 378 615 (car park, open Sundays)
O.S. Map: 151

ACCESS
Open at all times. Keep to the paths. Park safely at roadside if car park is closed.

HABITAT
Disused limestone workings, creating ponds, grassland, scrub and woodland.

STATUS
SSSI in the care of Warwickshire Wildlife Trust and Warwickshire County Council.

TARGET SPECIES
Dingy Skipper (*Erynnis tages*); Grizzled Skipper (*Pyrgus malvae*); Marbled White (*Melanargia galathea*); Small Blue (*Cupido minimus*); Brown Argus (*Aricia agestis*); White-letter Hairstreak (*Strymonidia w-album*) and Purple Hairstreak (*Quercusia quercus*).

TIMING
May week 4 to June week 2 for Small Blue, Grizzled Skipper, Dingy Skipper and Brown Argus, also August weeks 2 to 4 for Brown Argus. All July for Marbled White, July weeks 1 to 3 for White-letter Hairstreak and July week 3 to August week 2 for Purple Hairstreak.

OTHER SPECIES
Wall Brown (*Lasiommata megera*), which is scarce in the area, is present. Twenty-six species of butterflies and good numbers of common *Odonata* have been recorded.

OTHER FLORA AND FAUNA
Woodland birds are present in good numbers. The grasslands are species-rich with five orchid species recorded.

OTHER INFORMATION
A visit can be combined with one to Harbury Spoilbank Reserve nearby at SP 384 598, where similar species are present. A permit is required and is obtainable from Warwickshire Wildlife Trust, Brandon Marsh Nature Reserve, Brandon Lane, Coventry CV3 3GW.

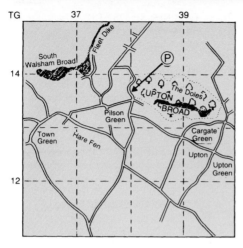

Grid Ref: TG 381 137
O.S. Map: 134

ACCESS
Contact NWT for permission to visit.

HABITAT
Open fen, alder carr and young oakwood.

STATUS
SSSI. Norfolk Wildlife Trust Nature Reserve.

TARGET SPECIES
Norfolk Hawker (*Aeshna isosceles*).

TIMING
June weeks 2 - 4.

OTHER SPECIES
Many of the common dragonfly species. White Admiral (*Ladoga camilla*) has occurred here.

OTHER FLORA AND FAUNA
Several rare species of orchid and sedge can be found on the reserve. Aquatic plants include Whorled Water-milfoil and Greater Bladderwort. Grass Snake present.

OTHER INFORMATION
Combine a visit here with one of the adjacent fens or Broads sites if time permits. The site is very boggy, so visitors should keep to the pathways.

Contact: Norfolk Wildlife Trust, 72 Cathedral Close, Norwich, Norfolk NR1 4DF.

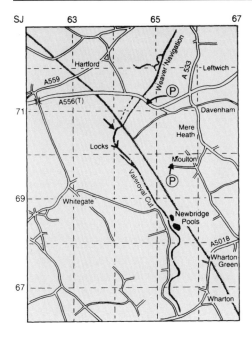

Grid Ref: SJ 641 706
O.S. Map: 118

ACCESS
Park along the A559 at SJ 648 712, east of the bridge, walk south along the west bank. Alternatively park in Moulton village and follow footpaths to the locks.

HABITAT
Well vegetated river bank and non-navigable loop of the River Weaver, backed by stands of mature, mainly deciduous trees.

TARGET SPECIES
Hairy Dragonfly (*Brachytron pratense*); Red-eyed Damselfly (*Erythromma najas*); Banded Demoiselle (*Calopteryx splendens*).

TIMING
June week 1 and 2, preferably prior to the start of the fishing season.

OTHER SPECIES
Migrant Hawker (*Aeshna mixta*) was recorded here in 1995, 1996 and 1997. Common *Odonata* occur in good numbers.

OTHER FLORA AND FAUNA
Grey Wagtail, common woodland birds.

OTHER INFORMATION
Do not park in any of the angler's car parks or drive down the road to the locks - these are all private. An information board near the lock keeper's cottage usually gives details of recent bird and dragonfly sightings.

Newbridge Pools at SJ 653 685, further down the Weaver near Winsford are also worth a visit. Migrant Hawker breeds here in good numbers.

TQ 17

Grid Ref: TQ 168 323 (car park)
O.S. Map: 187

ACCESS
Thursdays to Sundays 10am-6pm all
year. Small admission charge.

HABITAT
Lake, reeds, meadows, scrub and
woodland.

STATUS
Local Nature Reserve.

TARGET SPECIES
Red-eyed Damselfly (*Erythromma
najas*); Banded Demoiselle (*Calopteryx
splendens*); Brilliant Emerald
(*Somatochlora metallica*); Downy
Emerald (*Cordulia aenea*).

TIMING
June week 2 to July week 4 for Red-eyed Damselfly and Banded Demoiselle; June week 2
to July week 2 for Downy Emerald; July weeks 1 to 3 for Brilliant Emerald.

OTHER SPECIES
Eighteen species of *Odonata* and 23 butterflies have been recorded, including regular
Ringlet (*Aphantopus hyperantus*), Essex Skipper (*Thymelicus lineola*) and Purple
Hairstreak (*Quercusia quercus*).

OTHER FLORA AND FAUNA
Over 200 plant species have been recorded and a good cross-section of birds typical of the
habitat.

OTHER INFORMATION
Brilliant and Downy Emerald have been seen around the positions arrowed on the map.

Contact the reserve on 01403 256890 to check the status of the target species in the year of
the visit.

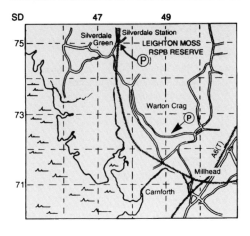

Grid Ref: SD 492 724 (car park)
O.S. Map: 97

ACCESS
Open access onto Warton Crag, east and north of the car park.

HABITAT
Limestone grassland and scrub.

STATUS
Lancashire Wildlife Trust Reserve.

TARGET SPECIES
Northern Brown Argus (*Aricia artaxerxes*); Grayling (*Hipparchia semele*); High Brown Fritillary (*Argynnis adippe*); Pearl-bordered Fritillary (*Boloria euphrosyne*); Small Pearl-bordered Fritillary (*Boloria selene*).

TIMING
May week 3 to June week 2 for Pearl-bordered Fritillary, June week 1 to July week 1 for Small Pearl-bordered Fritillary, and throughout July for High Brown Fritillary and Grayling. June week 2 to July week 2 for Northern Brown Argus.

OTHER SPECIES
A total of 33 butterfly species and 9 dragonfly species have been recorded within the Leighton Moss/Warton Crag complex. A total of 340 moth species have been recorded.

OTHER FLORA AND FAUNA
Orchids include Early Purple, Common Spotted and Common Twayblade.

OTHER INFORMATION
A visit can be combined with Leighton Moss RSPB Reserve at SD 478 751. Marsh Harrier, Bearded Tit and Bittern are present. Charge for non-members.

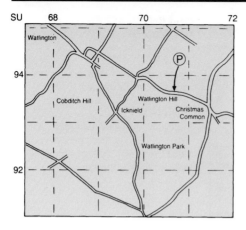

Grid Ref: SU 708 937 (car park)
O.S. Map: 175

ACCESS
Open access. Explore the area to the south of Watlington to Christmas Common road.

HABITAT
Chalk grassland.

STATUS
National Trust property.

TARGET SPECIES
Silver-spotted Skipper (*Hesperia comma*); Chalkhill Blue (*Lysandra coridon*).

TIMING
August weeks 2 to 4.

OTHER SPECIES
Several other common species occur.

OTHER INFORMATION
A visit to this site could be combined with one to Aston Rowant and to Bernwood Forest.

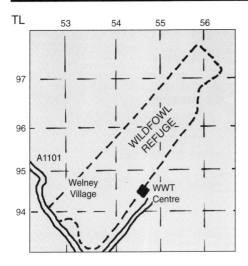

Grid Ref: TL 546 946
O.S. Map: 143

ACCESS
By permit obtainable from Welney WWT Centre. Parking available at Centre. Access from A1101.

HABITAT
Flood plain, grazing marsh. Reedbed, scrapes, willows and vegetated banks.

STATUS
WWT Nature Reserve. SSSI. Ramsar site.

TARGET SPECIES
Hairy Dragonfly (*Brachytron pratense*); Variable Damselfly (*Coenagrion pulchellum*); Scarce Chaser (*Libellula fulva*); Red-eyed Damselfly (*Erythromma najas*).

TIMING
May week 4 to June week 2 for Hairy Dragonfly; June weeks 2 to 4 for Scarce Chaser; June and July for Red-eyed Damselfly and Variable Damselfly.

OTHER SPECIES
Nineteen species of dragonfly annually recorded.

OTHER FLORA AND FAUNA
During spring/summer important breeding wader populations with numerous Lapwing, Redshank, Snipe, Ringed Plover and Little Ringed Plover. Marsh Harrier, Garganey, Avocet and Black-tailed Godwit seen regularly.

OTHER INFORMATION
Wheelchair access to much of the site. Summer walk, open June-September, depending upon breeding birds and flood levels, enables visitors to walk across part of washes.

Telephone for latest details 01353 680711. Visitors must keep to designated walkways.

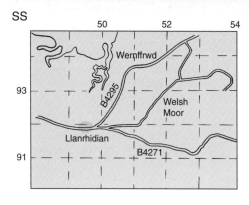

SS

Grid Ref: SS 520 927
O.S. Map: 159

ACCESS
Open access.

HABITAT
Acid grassland, heath and marsh.

STATUS
SSSI. Owned by National Trust.

TARGET SPECIES
Marsh Fritillary (*Eurodryas aurinia*); Small Pearl-bordered Fritillary (*Boloria selene*); Dingy Skipper (*Erynnis tages*).

TIMING
June weeks 1 to 3 for the target species.

OTHER SPECIES
Other common butterfly species are present.

OTHER INFORMATION
Welsh Moor is crossed by the minor road running south from the B4295 Wernffrwd to Llanrhidian road.

113. WHELDRAKE INGS National Nature Reserve, YORKSHIRE

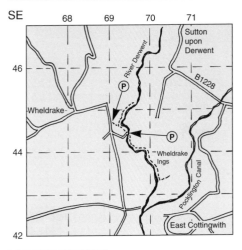

Grid Ref: SE 690 447 (car park at Bank Island)
SE 694 444 (car park by the River Derwent)
O.S. Map: 105

ACCESS
Public access along the public footpaths only.

HABITAT
Hay meadows and pasture by the River Derwent.

STATUS
National Nature Reserve managed by English Nature.

TARGET SPECIES
Ringlet (*Aphantopus hyperantus*); Small Skipper (*Thymelicus sylvestris*); Purple Hairstreak (*Quercusia quercus*); Brimstone (*Gonepteryx rhamni*); Banded Demoiselle (*Calopteryx splendens*); Red-eyed Damselfly (*Erythromma najas*).

TIMING
All June and July for Banded Demoiselle and Red-eyed Damselfly; April and September for Brimstone; July weeks 2 to 4 for Ringlet and Small Skipper and July week 3 to August week 2 for Purple Hairstreak.

OTHER SPECIES
Many common butterfly species occur and twenty-six species of dragonfly and damselfly have been recorded.

OTHER FLORA AND FAUNA
Nesting wildfowl and waders during spring and summer. In winter this is one of Britain's finest sites for swans, geese, ducks and waders.

OTHER INFORMATION
Red-veined Darter was recorded in 1996. Yellow-winged Darter was seen in 1995 and 1996. Hairy Dragonfly (*Brachytron pratense*) and Broad-bodied Chaser (*Libellula depressa*) have been recently recorded. Purple Hairstreak was seen in the trees by the River Derwent car park.

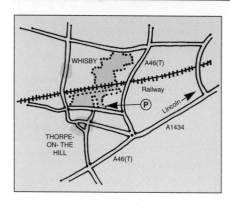

Grid Ref: SK 914 661
O.S. Map: 121

ACCESS
Public access.

HABITAT
Restored mineral workings with grassland and scrub.

STATUS
Lincolnshire Trust for Nature Conservation nature reserve.

TARGET SPECIES
Essex Skipper (*Thymelicus lineola*); Migrant Hawker (*Aeshna mixta*); Black-tailed Skimmer (*Orthetrum cancellatum*).

TIMING
June week 1 to July week 3 for Black-tailed Skimmer; August week 3 to September week 3 for Migrant Hawker; July week 4 to August week 3 for Essex Skipper.

OTHER SPECIES
Twenty species of dragonfly and damselfly and twenty-seven species of butterfly have been recorded at this site.

OTHER FLORA AND FAUNA
The site supports many species of bird typical of the habitat, including Sedge Warbler. Common Terns nest here and Goldeneye can be seen in the winter.

OTHER INFORMATION
Contact: Whisby Nature Park Warden, Moor Lane, Whisby, Lincolnshire. Tel: 01522 500676.

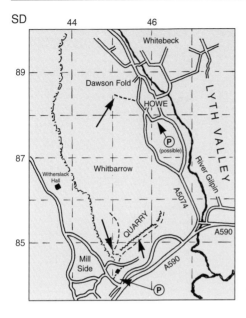

Grid Ref: SD 452 885 (for Duke of Burgundy)
O.S. Map: 97

ACCESS
Keep to the public footpath only. Park off the roads away from the village of Howe, where parking is virtually impossible. The land at the above reference is private, do not trespass.

HABITAT
Limestone grassland with scattered scrub and woodland.

TARGET SPECIES
Duke of Burgundy (*Hamearis lucina*) at one of its most northerly sites. High Brown Fritillary (*Argynnis adippe*); Silver-washed Fritillary (*Argynnis paphia*); Northern Brown Argus (*Aricia artaxerxes*); Small Pearl-bordered Fritillary (*Boloria selene*).

TIMING
May week 4 to June week 2 for Duke of Burgundy; all June for Small Pearl-bordered Fritillary; June week 3 to July week 2 for Northern Brown Argus; July weeks 2 to 4 for High Brown and Silver-washed Fritillaries.

OTHER SPECIES
Many common species of butterfly occur.

OTHER FLORA AND FAUNA
Fly Orchid, Limestone and Rigid Buckler Fern and typical northern limestone plants.

OTHER INFORMATION
The footpath to Lord's Seat from Howe village runs through the Duke of Burgundy site.

Silver-washed Fritillary is amazingly north of its main range!

Glades and slopes on the south side of the Scar are particularly good for fritillaries. Try areas around SD 453 847, 450 847 and 438 866.

A visit could also be combined with Cunsey Beck, Gait Barrows, Arnside Knott, Leighton Moss or Warton Crag.

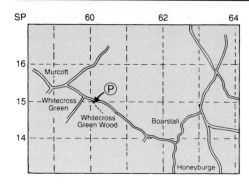

Grid Ref: SP 600 150
O.S. Map: 164

ACCESS
Open access along rides and footpaths.

HABITAT
Mixed woodland with well-vegetated rides.

STATUS
Berkshire, Buckinghamshire and Oxfordshire Naturalists Trust Nature Reserve.

TARGET SPECIES
Wood White (*Leptidea sinapis*).

TIMING
June weeks 1 to 3 for Wood White.

OTHER SPECIES
Many other common woodland species occur. Purple Emperor is now extremely hard to connect with at this site. Black Hairstreak (*Strymonidia pruni*) has been seen here.

OTHER FLORA AND FAUNA
Nightingale and Nightjar have bred.

OTHER INFORMATION
A visit could be combined with Bernwood Forest.

Contact: BBONT, 3 Church Cowley Road, Rose Hill, Oxford OX4 3JR.

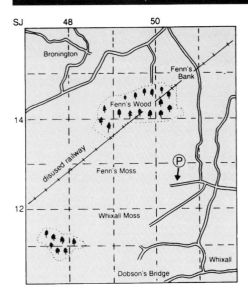

Grid Ref: SJ 505 125 (reserve car park)
O.S. Map: 126

ACCESS
Permit required from English Nature away from the perimeter footpaths.

HABITAT
Lowland raised mire.

STATUS
National Nature Reserve and SSSI owned and managed by English Nature.

TARGET SPECIES
Large Heath (*Coenonympha tullia*); White-faced Darter (*Leucorrhinia dubia*).

TIMING
June week 4 to July week 3 for Large Heath, June week 1 to July week 2 for White-faced Darter.

OTHER SPECIES
Several of the commoner species of dragonfly and butterfly can be seen on the site.

OTHER FLORA AND FAUNA
Some of Britain's scarcer plants such as Bog Rosemary and rare bog mosses occur on the SSSI. Bog Bush Cricket is also present.

OTHER INFORMATION
The site is owned or leased by English Nature and the Countryside Council for Wales. The mossland has previously been damaged by peat extraction and is now under repair.

Access to the site is allowed if a permit is obtained from the Site Manager, Manor House, Moss Lane, Whixall, Shropshire SY13 2PD.

Do not stray off the paths onto the fragile moss itself. A permit is necessary if Large Heath and White-faced Darter are to be looked for.

A visit here can be combined with Prees Heath.

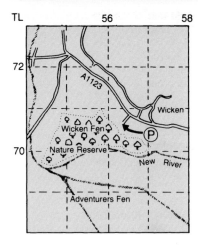

Grid Ref: TL 563 705
O.S. Map: 154

ACCESS
Public access to boardwalk trail and Tower Hide at all times.

HABITAT
A mosaic of habitats are present on the various fens in the complex, from large artificial lake, ditch systems, reedbeds and 'carr' woodland.

STATUS
SSSI. National Nature Reserve, owned by the National Trust.

TARGET SPECIES
Hairy Dragonfly (*Brachytron pratense*); Emperor Dragonfly (*Anax imperator*); Black-tailed Skimmer (*Orthetrum cancellatum*); Variable Damselfly (*Coenagrion pulchellum*); Red-eyed Damselfly (*Erythromma najas*).

TIMING
A visit in June weeks 1 and 2 will coincide with Hairy Dragonfly, Black-tailed Skimmer, Red-eyed and Variable Damselflies. June week 4 to July week 4 for Emperor Dragonfly and the previous species bar Hairy Dragonfly.

OTHER SPECIES
Eighteen species of dragonfly and damselfly have been recorded on the reserve. Many common butterfly species also occur.

OTHER FLORA AND FAUNA
Fen Violet, Greater Butterwort and many other fenland species. Birds include Marsh Harrier, Bearded Tit and Bittern.

OTHER INFORMATION
Admission is free to National Trust members, but there is a charge to non-members.

The Swallowtail re-introduction scheme is not continuing at the moment.

Contact: The Warden, Wicken Fen, Lode Lane, Wicken, Ely, Cambridgeshire. Dragonfly leaflet available.

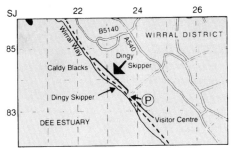

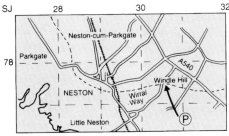

Grid Ref: SJ 238 835
THURSTASTON VISITOR CENTRE
SJ 306 776 NESTON
O.S. Map: 108 and 107

ACCESS
Public access along the Wirral Way footpath.

HABITAT
Disused railway line with grassland, scrub and some mature woodland bordering.

STATUS
Country Park managed by Wirral Ranger Service.

TARGET SPECIES
Dingy Skipper (*Erynnis tages*), which is rare in the area, at Thurstaston; Purple Hairstreak (*Quercusia quercus*) and White-letter Hairstreak (*Strymonidia w-album*) at Neston.

TIMING
May week 4 to June week 3 for Dingy Skipper. July week 1 to 3 for White-letter Hairstreak. July week 3 to August week 2 for Purple Hairstreak.

OTHER SPECIES
Many common butterflies for the area can be seen.

OTHER FLORA AND FAUNA
A wide variety of plants and birds can be seen along the Wirral Way and on the Dee Estuary, depending upon the time of a visit.

OTHER INFORMATION
Dingy Skipper has a couple of colonies on the disused railway line north of Thurstaston Visitor Centre as far as Simon's Bridge. The hairstreaks at Neston are adjacent to the parking areas in the Oaks and Elms.

Contact: Wirral Ranger Service, Thurstaston Visitor Centre, Thurstaston, Wirral.

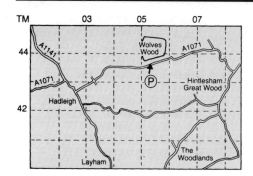

Grid Ref: TM 054 440
O.S. Map: 155

ACCESS
Public access. Park in reserve car park at TM 054 436.

HABITAT
Ancient woodland.

STATUS
RSPB Nature Reserve, SSSI.

TARGET SPECIES
White-letter Hairstreak (*Strymonidia w-album*); Purple Hairstreak (*Quercusia quercus*); Essex Skipper (*Thymelicus lineola*).

TIMING
July week 1 to July week 3 for White-letter Hairstreak, July week 3 to August week 2 for Purple Hairstreak, July week 4 to August week 3 for Essex Skipper.

OTHER SPECIES
Many common butterfly species occur.

OTHER FLORA AND FAUNA
Birds in the wood include Nightingale, four species of warbler, Great and Lesser Spotted Woodpeckers and occasionally Hawfinch. Plants include Herb Paris and Yellow Archangel indicating the wood's ancient origins.

OTHER INFORMATION
Please follow the waymarked trail from the car park.

138

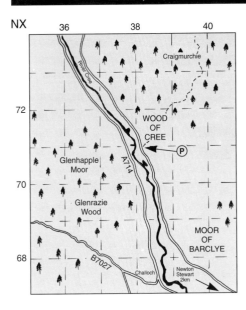

Grid Ref: NX 382 709 (parking)
O.S. Map: 77 and 83

ACCESS
Open, keeping to footpaths.

HABITAT
Oak wood, streams and moorland.

STATUS
RSPB Reserve.

TARGET SPECIES
Small Pearl-bordered Fritillary (*Boloria selene*); Dark Green Fritillary (*Argynnis aglaja*); Scotch Argus (*Erebia aethiops*); Purple Hairstreak (*Quercusia quercus*).

TIMING
All June for Small Pearl-bordered Fritillary; July weeks 2 to 4 for Dark Green Fritillary; August weeks 1 to 3 for Scotch Argus and Purple Hairstreak.

OTHER SPECIES
Typical *Odonata* species for the area and habitat occur in good numbers. Large Skipper (*Ochlodes venata*) and Wall (*Lasiommata megera*), both towards the northern edge of their range, occur.

OTHER FLORA AND FAUNA
Wood Warbler, Redstart, Tree Pipit and Pied Flycatcher are all present. Typical plant species of the habitat occur.

OTHER INFORMATION
One of the largest populations of Purple Hairstreak in Scotland.

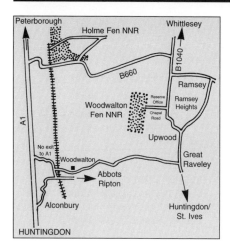

Grid Ref: TL 234 848 (entrance)
O.S. Map: 142

ACCESS
Permit only

HABITAT
Fenland, open water, woodland and wet heath.

STATUS
National Nature Reserve.

TARGET SPECIES
Hairy Dragonfly (*Brachytron pratense*);
Scarce Chaser (*Libellula fulva*).

TIMING
May week 3 to June week 2 for Hairy Dragonfly, June for Scarce Chaser.

OTHER SPECIES
Other less common species including Red-eyed Damselfly (*Erythromma najas*) are present. Nineteen of the 24 recorded species are regularly seen. Common butterflies occur but the Large Copper introduced here, is effectively extinct. Sixteen butterfly species were recorded on transects in 1996.

OTHER FLORA AND FAUNA
Over 400 plant species have been recorded on the reserve including Fen Violet and Fen Woodrush. Chinese Water Deer are present.

OTHER INFORMATION
This is one of the finest reserves in Britain. A visit could be combined Holme Fen NNR just 4 km from Woodwalton. This reserve is open access but keep to the paths. Entry from the roads crossing the reserve around TL 204 896 or TL 215 887.

Contact: English Nature, Bedfordshire, Cambridgeshire and Northamptonshire Team, Ham Lane House, Ham Lane, Orton Waterville, Peterborough PE2 5UR.

SK

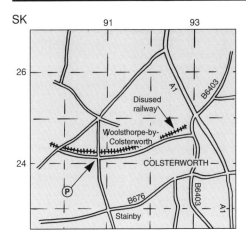

Grid Ref: SK 929 249 to 902 242
O.S. Map: 130

ACCESS
Park at Stainby crossroads.

HABITAT
Disused railway line.

STATUS
Lincolnshire Trust for Nature
Conservation nature reserve.

TARGET SPECIES
Grizzled Skipper (*Pyrgus malvae*) and
Dingy Skipper (*Erynnis tages*).

TIMING
May week 2 to June week 1 for Grizzled Skipper and May week 4 to June week 3 for
Dingy Skipper.

OTHER SPECIES
Many other common butterfly species can be encountered on the site.

OTHER INFORMATION
For further information contact the Lincolnshire Trust for Nature Conservation,
Banovallum House, Manor House Street, Horncastle, Lincolnshire LN9 5HF.

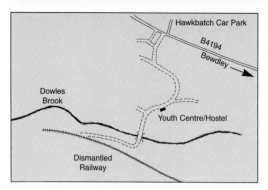

Grid Ref: SO 762 777 (car park)
O.S. Map: 138

ACCESS
Numerous public tracks. The old railway track should not be missed. Access to the Wyre Forest is also available from the A456 Bewdley to Tenbury Wells road.

HABITAT
Wyre Forest of 2,634 hectares is one of the largest surviving areas of woodland on an ancient woodland site in Great Britain. There are, in addition, areas of unimproved grassland, old orchards and several streams.

STATUS
Part National Nature Reserve, SSSI, part Forest Nature Reserve.

TARGET SPECIES
Wood White (*Leptidea sinapis*); Pearl-bordered Fritillary (*Bolora euphrosyne*); Small Pearl-bordered Fritillary (*Boloria selene*); White Admiral (*Ladoga camilla*); Silver-washed Fritillary (*Argynnis paphia*); White-letter Hairstreak (*Strymonidia w-album*); Purple Hairstreak (*Quercusia quercus*); Dingy Skipper (*Erynnis tages*); Grizzled Skipper (*Pyrgus malvae*).

TIMING
May week 4 to June week 2 for Dingy Skipper, Grizzled Skipper, Pearl-bordered Fritillary and Wood White. All June for Small Pearl-bordered Fritillary. July weeks 1 to 3 for White-letter Hairstreak and White Admiral. July week 3 to August week 1 for Silver-washed Fritillary and Purple Hairstreak.

OTHER SPECIES
Total list of 34 butterfly species including possible High Brown Fritillary (*Argynnis adippe*). Excellent range of dragonflies owing to variety of habitats.

OTHER FLORA AND FAUNA
The forest is one of the few British localities for the terrestrial Caddis Fly (*Enoicyla pustilla*). The hay meadows found within the forest contain a range of orchids, including Green-winged. Meadow Saffron can also be seen. Very good woodland bird community, including all three woodpeckers in addition to Redstart and Pied Flycatcher. Dowles Brook is a very good site for both Dipper and Kingfisher. Fallow Deer can often be seen within the forest glades.

OTHER INFORMATION
Large visitor centre signed of the A456. A site visit could be combined with visits to Trench Wood or Monkwood. However, the site has numerous habitats to explore and one or two days can easily be used constructively.

Contact: John Robinson/Michael Taylor, English Nature, Lodge Hill Farm, Dowles Brook, Bewdley DY12 2LY.

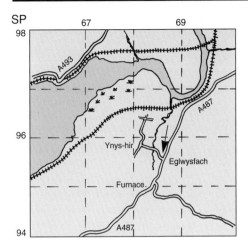

Grid Ref: SN 685 955 (reserve entrance)
O.S. Map: 135

ACCESS
Public access along the paths during reserve opening hours from 9.00 am.

HABITAT
Woodland, moorland, estuary and saltmarsh.

STATUS
RSPB Nature Reserve.

TARGET SPECIES
Small Pearl-bordered Fritillary (*Boloria selene*); Dark Green Fritillary (*Argynnis aglaja*); Purple Hairstreak (*Quercusia quercus*); Beautiful Demoiselle (*Calopteryx virgo*); Golden-ringed Dragonfly (*Cordulegaster boltonii*).

TIMING
All June for Small Pearl-bordered Fritillary, June week 3 to July week 4 for Beautiful Demoiselle and Golden-ringed Dragonfly, July week 3 to August week 1 for Dark Green Fritillary and Purple Hairstreak.

OTHER SPECIES
Silver-washed Fritillary (*Argynnis paphia*) occurs occasionally. Thirteen species of *Odonata* have been recorded.

OTHER FLORA AND FAUNA
Notable for breeding birds which include Pied Flycatcher, Redstart and Common Buzzard. Red Kite sometimes seen.

OTHER INFORMATION
Up to the minute information is available at the reception centre. Charge for non-RSPB members. Contact: Dick Squires, Cae'r Berllan, Eglwys-fach, Machynlleth, Powys, SY20 8TA. Tel: 01654 781265.

ACCIDENTAL AND VAGRANT BUTTERFLIES

Annually occurring visitors have been dealt with under the site guides section of the book and included in the checklists and flight period tables. The non-annually occurring or vagrant and accidental species are dealt with in this short section.

Scarce Swallowtail
There have been very few records of this species, although at least one was claimed in 1995.

Pale Clouded Yellow
This species is occasionally recorded in Clouded Yellow years, but care needs to be taken not to confuse the pale form of Clouded Yellow with this much rarer butterfly. In 1947, 870 were recorded and several were reported from the south coast in 1995.

Berger's Clouded Yellow
Even rarer than the above species, Berger's Clouded Yellow have occurred in years when there has been an invasion of Clouded Yellows.

Bath White
Small numbers of this rare migrant are recorded most years in S.E. England.

Long-tailed Blue
This extremely rare migrant has only been recorded in small numbers. Reports were received of individuals in Devon in 1995.

American Painted Lady
At least one was seen at Prawle Point in Devon in 1995 and several other probables were reported. Prior to 1995 there were fewer than 20 records of American Painted Lady.

Camberwell Beauty
1995 was an excellent year for this species with many tens, perhaps hundreds, recorded. The first wave of records occurred in early August in Norfolk, Kent and surprisingly, Cheshire. Over the next few weeks reports were received from several counties throughout England, the butterflies often feeding on fallen fruit or Buddleia bushes.

Monarch or Milkweed
As with the above species 1995 was an exceptional year for this vagrant. During October many individuals were reported from the south-west, coinciding with an arrival of American rare birds to the Scilly Isles.

Queen of Spain Fritillary
A rare migrant favouring rough ground, usually recorded in S.E. England. During 1996 and 1997 this species occurred at a number of sites in Suffolk and has bred.

ACCIDENTAL AND VAGRANT DRAGONFLIES

Most species of *Odonata* are sedentary in the United Kingdom. Only the Migrant Hawker is known to migrate here on a regular basis. However several species have made it to the shores of the UK in recent years, 1995 being a particularly good year. Several new records for the UK were reported along with large numbers of rarer species.

Vagrant Emperor
Singles have been recorded in recent years inland in Leeds and Cambridge and on the Isle of Man in 1995. Two were recorded in 1996.

Scarlet Darter
One seen in 1995 in Cornwall on August 7th, will, if accepted, be a new species for the UK. This species is common in France, so it is not surprising that it is now a likely addition to the British list. Another was recorded in 1997.

Banded Darter
Another addition to the British list in 1995 when one was seen and photographed in Dyfed on August 16th and 17th.

Yellow-winged Darter
Prior to 1995 there had only been a handful of records of this species, but in August 1995 the start of a major invasion was noted in Great Yarmouth Cemetery. By August 3rd as many as 600 were present. Over the following weeks Yellow-winged Darters were recorded in almost 30 counties from as far north as Lancashire and into Mid-Glamorgan and Dyfed. Full details of the invasion are given by Jill Silsby in the British Dragonfly Society Autumn 1995 Newsletter. There was some evidence of successful breeding at a few sites.

Red-veined Darter
This species is an irregular immigrant, but in 1995 several individuals were associated with the Darter invasion, including a scattering of records in Cornwall. The following year this species occurred widely and bred at at least one site.

Vagrant Darter
Several specimens of Vagrant Darter were reported in 1995, including four in Great Yarmouth Cemetery and two in Middlesex.

Southern Skimmer
An unconfirmed report for 1995 concerns one on Dartmoor on August 8th, but it could not be relocated the following day.

Lesser Emperor
This species, new for Britain, was recorded in Gloucestershire in mid-June 1996. There were two further records in 1997.

ESCAPES, RELEASES AND RE-INTRODUCTIONS

With the vast interest that exists in butterflies, it is inevitable that escapes from butterfly houses and private collections are going to happen. On the whole these refer to species from hotter climes than the UK and do not pose a serious threat to the country's natural butterfly populations. Unfortunately the same cannot be said for the numerous releases that are undertaken illegally, without an official license and often without sufficient forethought into how the release will affect the native populations. It is beyond the scope of this publication to deal with the pros and cons of releasing butterflies, but it does make the serious matter of butterfly recording more difficult when species turn up miles away from their traditional sites.

For some species in the UK, the true status is not known or understood. Every year Large Tortoiseshells and Maps are recorded in the UK. These may refer to illegal releases, but could refer to genuine vagrants or to still undiscovered colonies.

Well planned re-introductions have been carried out by English Nature and Butterfly Conservation in recent years. All of these projects have been well planned with the reasons behind decline or extinction determined and the relevant action taken to ensure that the site used for the re-introduction is suitable for the species concerned. Stock from genetically similar, self-sustaining populations, are used and the results monitored for several years.

Species that are currently the subject of such schemes, under English Nature's Species Recovery Programme are Large Blue in the West Country and more recently Chequered Skipper in the Midlands. As the details of these sites are still confidential, we have not included them in the book. Should a site become open to the public, details will be carried (with the landowner's permission) in future editions.

Some branches of Butterfly Conservation are actively involved in attempts to re-establish certain species to areas where they have become extinct. Other species that have been the subject of re-introduction programmes which have failed, have included, the Large Copper at Woodwalton Fen. In all cases of re-introductions an Action Plan has to be prepared, detailing the current status of the species, main threats to its continued survival, objectives of the project and broad policies. Proposed actions, safeguarding the site and land acquisition, subsequent management and species protection are also fully considered.

Further information on butterfly re-introductions can be found in John Feltwell's "The Conservation of British Butterflies," which summarises the Large Blue, Large Copper and Swallowtail schemes.

BUTTERFLY CONSERVATION

Founded in 1968 Butterfly Conservation now has a membership of over 10,000 and a network of 26 regional branches throughout the country from Cornwall to the Highlands and from Northern Ireland to Norfolk.

The Society is run mostly by volunteers with assistance from a small professional team of conservation and administrative staff. They have extensive experience in co-ordinating a number of projects and campaigns to conserve butterflies.

Many of the UK's 56 butterfly species are threatened by extinction or are in rapid decline owing to changes in agricultural practice, forestry or increased urbanisation. Butterfly Conservation is working to halt this decline and to save threatened species.

In 1994 Butterfly Conservation launched the Land Rover Woodlands Campaign — "New Life for Old Woodlands". The campaign sets out to reverse the trends that caused the decline of many of our woodland species and encourages diverse woodlands that are full of butterflies.

1995 saw the launch of "Action for Butterflies" — a project aimed at providing a sound national framework to reverse butterfly decline and produce Species Action Plans for 25 threatened species.

Butterfly Conservation owns or manages several wildlife reserves, many of which are featured in this book. In addition to this work, members liaise closely with a wide range of public and private bodies in evolving local and national conservation policies and in managing land for butterflies.

Members of the various branches of Butterfly Conservation organise numerous field trips and indoor meetings throughout the year. They also help with conservation work such as surveying, wardening and land management. Their junior section is called the "Chrysalis Club" and an education pack has been produced for teachers as part of the national curriculum. Members also receive "Butterfly News", the society's own A4 colour magazine, three times a year and local newsletters.

Details of membership are available from Butterfly Conservation, PO Box 222, Dedham, Colchester, Essex CO7 6EY.

**BUTTERFLY
CONSERVATION**

BRITISH DRAGONFLY SOCIETY

The British Dragonfly Society is the UK's only charity devoted to the conservation of our *Odonata*. Membership is open to anyone with an interest in Dragonflies or who would like to be involved in their conservation. Members receive two copies of the society's journal and newsletter each year. During the summer, field trips throughout the country are organised and led by the society. At the end of the year the AGM contains talks and discussions on a wide variety of dragonfly topics, most of which are illustrated by slides or exhibits.

The organisation has a very active Dragonfly Conservation Group who act as advisors on odonatological matters to English Nature, The Environment Agency, County Wildlife Trusts, the RSPB and Butterfly Conservation. Members of the group make themselves available for consultation on conservation matters where and when required. The following page gives details of the network of regional recorders who collate dragon and damselfly records before forwarding them to the national recorder. This information, for all sites, is valuable when trying to protect sites or offer conservation advice.

Financial assistance is given (when possible) to other conservation bodies working on projects that will benefit dragonflies. Advice is given to landowners, conservation officers, reserve wardens and members of the public. They encourage the excavation of ponds and the maintenance of streams, canals, marshes and other areas where dragonflies should be able to develop. To this end they have published two illustrated booklets, *'Dig a Pond for Dragonflies'* and *'Managing Habitats for Dragonflies'*.

Other publications produced include the twice yearly *'Journal of the British Dragonfly Society'* which contains articles on *Odonata* that have been recorded from the British Isles. This, along with a twice yearly topical newsletter, which includes details of the many field trips and meetings organised, is distributed free to members. Back copies of the journal are available. A dragonfly fact sheet, intended for young members of the public is available.

A large identification Chart of British Dragonflies is available from the secretary.

For further information, or to join BDS, write to: Jill Silsby, 1 Haydn Avenue, Purley, Surrey CR8 4AG.

BRITISH DRAGONFLY SOCIETY REGIONAL RECORDERS

NORTH ENGLAND	Mr D. Clarke, Burnfoot, Cumwhitton, Carlisle CA4 9EX
MID-EAST ENGLAND	Mr S. A. Chan, 45 Weltmore Road, Luton, Bedfordshire LU3 2TN
SOUTH-WEST ENGLAND	Mr D. C. Winsland, 2 Starfield Road, West Southbourne, Bournemouth BH5 2AR
SOUTH-EAST ENGLAND	Mr A. R. Welstead, 3 Kelvin Close, Hythe, Southampton SO4 5LW
SCOTLAND	Mrs E. M. Smith, 33 Hunter Terrace, Loanhead, Midlothian EH20 9JS
WALES	Mrs S. Coker, ''Mountain', Clarbeston Road, Haverfordwest, Dyfed SA63 4SG
IRELAND	Mr B. Nelson, 84 Drumnagoon Road, Portadown, Co Armagh BT63 5RF

USEFUL ADDRESSES

British Butterfly Conservation Society
PO Box 222, Dedham, Colchester, Essex CO7 6EY

British Dragonfly Society
c/o Jill Silsby, 1 Haydn Avenue, Purley, Surrey CR8 4AG

Royal Society for the Protection of Birds
The Lodge, Sandy, Bedfordshire SG19 2DL

Wildlife Trusts Partnership (RSNC)
Witham Park, Waterside South, Lincoln, Lincolnshire LN5 7JR

PHOTOGRAPHY

The authors are experienced photographers who give slide shows regularly to the general public.

Undoubtedly the most suitable camera for general photography of dragonflies and butterflies is a single lens reflex (SLR). It should possess at least manual and aperture priority metering. The choice of lens is critical. A 90mm macro, is very versatile and allows use for general photography. However they are quite expensive.

Many people will already possess a camera with a standard (50mm) lens or a short zoom such as a 28mm-80mm. Some of these zooms have a macro facility which is useful for larger insects. The general drawback with these lenses is that they will not focus on close subjects.

To avoid this problem extension rings can be used between the lens and the camera body. They contain no lenses and are quite cheap to buy. The rings often come in sets of three different sizes and can be used singly or in combination. The smallest ring is used most frequently.

Possibly less effective is a 2x macro-converter. Unlike rings they contain lenses and considerably cut down the available light reaching the film. They are also more expensive than extension rings.

Depth of field, which is the amount of the subject in sharp focus, is critical with macro-photography. A top view of a butterfly with open wings causes few problems but photographed from another angle it would be difficult to get the subject fully in focus. A depth of field preview button on some SLR's enables the photographer to view exactly how much of the picture is in sharp focus.

An aperture of f22 provides a great depth of field but when the aperture is widened down f2.8 the depth of field is considerably reduced. Depth of field can be frequently used to allow the photographer to manipulate the picture. For instance, it can be used to blur out a distracting background.

To have a greater opportunity to manipulate shutter speed and aperture to best advantage, a fast film is a great aid. A 400 ISO film is much faster than a 50 ISO film. There is however no gain without pain as the film is more expensive and picture quality slightly grainier. However a 400 ISO film is certainly a good all-round choice for use in the UK.

Dark subjects against a light background and vice-versa causes problems when operating on the automatic function. The dark and light subjects can lose definition by under and over exposure. A camera with spot metering can avoid this. Switching to the manual function and adjusting controls appropriately will do the job but loss of background definition is an inevitable result.

Many of the problems of using natural light can be avoided by the employment of flash. Many photographers prefer to use two flash guns mounted either side of the camera to avoid harsh lighting and strong shadows. Although the shutter speed is usually set slow the electronic flash will give a sharp image, with few camera shake problems and a good depth of field.

This type of photography at first is a little 'hit and miss' until the correct speed and aperture are found. Keep notes of the trial shots until you get it right.

It is not too difficult to obtain documentary photographs of butterflies and dragonflies but very hard to achieve anything 'artistic'. The real satisfaction comes in the shot which fully describes the species in its habitat but looks beautiful as well. Try to be inventive in approach, perhaps shooting against the light or from below. Indeed try anything to make the shot unusual.

The importance of fieldcraft cannot be stressed greatly enough! Subjects will often land on a favourite perch or flower, so patience is important whilst waiting for them to oblige. Rather than moving the hand forward to the focusing ring which may disturb the subject it is better to pre-focus and move in physically until the subject comes into focus. Be wary of the sun's position. Use a lens hood if possible and avoid casting shadows over the subject or moving the surrounding vegetation.

Some form of support for the camera may be useful, but most camera tripods do not allow for low-level photography. Three manufacturers produce 'professional' tripods that are excellent for macro and low-level photography. Tripods however tend to be cumbersome in the field, unless your subject is a recently emerged specimen and you have the time to set up the tripod and camera. A much more realistic option is a monopod with a ball and socket. This will help steady the camera, while still allowing you to set up quickly and move around.

Finally be prepared to use lots of film and bear in mind that good photographs are often obtained after many patient hours of waiting.

Our standard equipment comprises:

Pentax bodies with motor-drives	Plenty of film
Tamron SP2 24-48 f3.5 lens	Polythene sheet - for lying on in wet grass
Tamron 90mm f2.8 macro lens	Lens cleaning clothes and brushes
Set of three extension rings	Jeweller's screwdrivers (in case of repairs)
2x KAX Macro Teleplus MC7 Converter	Manfrotto MN055 tripod with MN141 head
Spare batteries for camera and motor-drives	Manfrotto MN079B monopod
	Cobra haversack camera bag

CHECKLIST OF BRITISH BUTTERFLIES

Species		1	2	3	4	5	6	7	8
HESPERIIDAE									
Chequered Skipper	*Carterocephalus palaemon*								
Small Skipper	*Thymelicus sylvestris*								
Essex Skipper	*T. lineola*								
Lulworth Skipper	*T. acteon*								
Silver-spotted Skipper	*Hesperia comma*								
Large Skipper	*Ochlodes venata*								
Dingy Skipper	*Erynnis tages*								
Grizzled Skipper	*Pyrgus malvae*								

Species		1	2	3	4	5	6	7	8
PAPILIONIDAE									
Swallowtail	*Papilio machaon*								

Species		1	2	3	4	5	6	7	8
PIERIDAE									
Wood White	*Leptidea sinapis*								
Clouded Yellow	*Colias croceus*								
Brimstone	*Gonepteryx rhamni*								
Large White	*Pieris brassicae*								
Small White	*P. rapae*								
Green-veined White	*P. napi*								
Orange Tip	*Anthocaris cardamines*								

Species		1	2	3	4	5	6	7	8
LYCAENIDAE									
Green Hairstreak	*Callophrys rubi*								
Brown Hairstreak	*Thecla betulae*								
Purple Hairstreak	*Quercusia quercus*								
White-letter Hairstreak	*Strymonidia w-album*								
Black Hairstreak	*S. pruni*								
Small Copper	*Lycaena phlaeas*								
Small Blue	*Cupido minimus*								
Silver-studded Blue	*Plebejus argus*								
Brown Argus	*Aricia agesis*								
Northern Brown Argus	*A. artaxerxes*								
Common Blue	*Polyommatus icarus*								
Chalkhill Blue	*Lysandra coridon*								
Adonis Blue	*L. bellargus*								
Holly Blue	*Celastrina argiolus*								

Species		1	2	3	4	5	6	7	8
NEMEOBIIDAE									
Duke of Burgundy	*Hamearis lucina*								

NYMPHALIDAE									
White Admiral	*Ladoga camilla*								
Purple Emperor	*Apatura iris*								
Red Admiral	*Vanessa atalanta*								
Painted Lady	*Cynthia cardui*								
Small Tortoiseshell	*Aglais urticae*								
Peacock	*Inachis io*								
Comma	*Polygonia c-album*								
Small Pearl-bordered Fritillary	*Boloria selene*								
Pearl-bordered Fritillary	*B. euphrosyne*								
High Brown Fritillary	*Argynnis adippe*								
Dark Green Fritillary	*A. aglaja*								
Silver-washed Fritillary	*A. paphia*								
Marsh Fritillary	*Eurodryas aurinia*								
Glanville Fritillary	*Melitaea cinxia*								
Heath Fritillary	*Mellicta athalia*								

SATYRIDAE									
Speckled Wood	*Pararge aegeria*								
Wall	*Lasiommata megera*								
Mountain Ringlet	*Erebia epiphron*								
Scotch Argus	*E. aethiops*								
Marbled White	*Melanargia galathea*								
Grayling	*Hipparchia semele*								
Gatekeeper	*Pyronia tithonus*								
Meadow Brown	*Maniola jurtina*								
Small Heath	*Coenonympha pamphilus*								
Large Heath	*C. tullia*								
Ringlet	*Aphantopus hyperantus*								

CHECKLIST OF BRITISH DRAGONFLIES & DAMSELFLIES

Species		1	2	3	4	5	6	7	8

ZYGOPTERA

PLATYCNEMIDIDAE

| White-legged Damselfly | *Platycnemis pennipes* | | | | | | | | |

COENAGRIIDAE

Small Red Damselfly	*Ceriagrion tenellum*								
Red-eyed Damselfly	*Erythromma najas*								
Northern Damselfly	*Coenagrion hastulatum*								
Southern Damselfly	*C. mercuriale*								
Azure Damselfly	*C. puella*								
Variable Damselfly	*C. pulchellum*								
Common Blue Damselfly	*Enallagma cyathigerum*								
Large Red Damselfly	*Pyrrhosoma nymphula*								
Blue-tailed Damselfly	*Ischnura elegans*								
Scarce Blue-tailed Damselfly	*I. pumilio*								

LESTIDAE

| Scarce Emerald Damselfly | *Lestes dryas* | | | | | | | | |
| Emerald Damselfly | *L. sponsa* | | | | | | | | |

CALOPTERYGIDAE

| Banded Demoiselle | *Calopteryx splendens* | | | | | | | | |
| Beautiful Demoiselle | *C. virgo* | | | | | | | | |

Species		1	2	3	4	5	6	7	8

ANISOPTERA

GOMPHIDAE

| Club-tailed Dragonfly | *Gomphus vulgatissimus* |

AESHNIDAE

Hairy Dragonfly	*Brachytron pratense*
Azure Hawker	*Aeshna caerulea*
Southern Hawker	*A. cyanea*
Brown Hawker	*A. grandis*
Norfolk Hawker	*A. isosceles*
Common Hawker	*A. juncea*
Migrant Hawker	*A. mixta*
Emperor Dragonfly	*Anax imperator*

CORDULEGASTERIDAE

| Golden-ringed Dragonfly | *Cordulegaster boltonii* |

CORDULIIDAE

Downy Emerald	*Cordulia aenea*
Northern Emerald	*Somatochlora arctica*
Brilliant Emerald	*S. metallica*

LIBELLULIDAE

Black-tailed Skimmer	*Orthetrum cancellatum*
Keeled Skimmer	*O. coerulescens*
Broad-bodied Chaser	*Libellula depressa*
Scarce Chaser	*L. fulva*
Four-spotted Chaser	*L. quadrimaculata*
Black Darter	*Sympetrum danae*
Highland Darter	*S. nigrescens*
Ruddy Darter	*S. sanguineum*
Common Darter	*S. striolatum*
White-faced Darter	*Leucorrhinia dubia*

BRITISH BUTTERFLY FLIGHT PERIODS

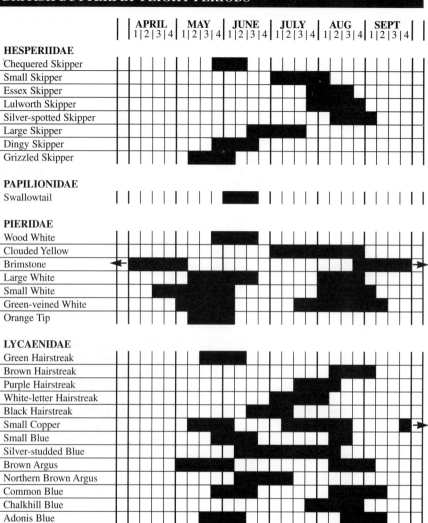

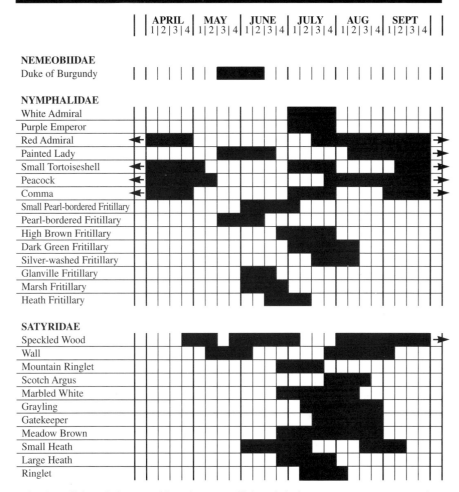

The above flight periods are a guide to the average flight periods, in some years emergence may be earlier and in others later. Some species, in favourable years, may be triple brooded, while others will only produce a second brood in favourable years. Species which hibernate as adults (Small Tortoiseshell and Peacock for example) can be seen in any month and will emerge from hibernation if the temperature increases.

BRITISH DAMSELFLY FLIGHT PERIODS

	MAY	JUNE	JULY	AUG	SEPT
	3 4	1 2 3 4	1 2 3 4	1 2 3 4	1 2 3 4

PLATYCNEMIDIDAE
White-legged Damselfly

COENAGRIIDAE
Small Red Damselfly
Red-eyed Damselfly
Northern Damselfly
Southern Damselfly
Azure Damselfly
Variable Damselfly
Common Blue Damselfly
Large Red Damselfly
Blue-tailed Damselfly
Scarce Blue-tailed Damselfly

LESTIDAE
Scarce Emerald Damselfly
Emerald Damselfly

CALOPTERYGIDAE
Banded Demoiselle
Beautiful Demoiselle

BRITISH DRAGONFLY FLIGHT PERIODS

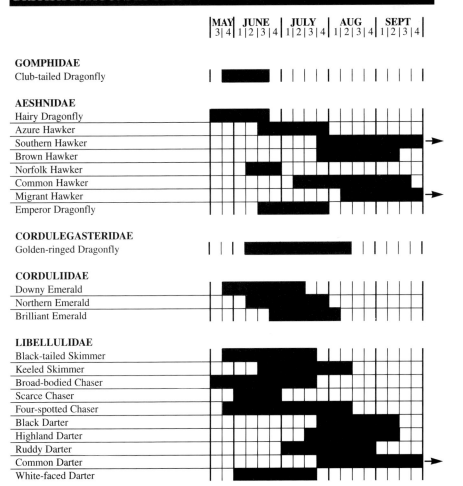

	MAY		JUNE			JULY				AUG				SEPT			
	3	4	1	2	3	4	1	2	3	4	1	2	3	4	1	2	3	4

GOMPHIDAE
Club-tailed Dragonfly

AESHNIDAE
Hairy Dragonfly
Azure Hawker
Southern Hawker
Brown Hawker
Norfolk Hawker
Common Hawker
Migrant Hawker
Emperor Dragonfly

CORDULEGASTERIDAE
Golden-ringed Dragonfly

CORDULIIDAE
Downy Emerald
Northern Emerald
Brilliant Emerald

LIBELLULIDAE
Black-tailed Skimmer
Keeled Skimmer
Broad-bodied Chaser
Scarce Chaser
Four-spotted Chaser
Black Darter
Highland Darter
Ruddy Darter
Common Darter
White-faced Darter

Odonata flight periods may vary somewhat, depending on climatic conditions, from year to year.

159

REFERENCES & BIBLIOGRAPHY

BBCS Merseyside Branch, *Butterflies of Merseyside*

Bedfordshire, Buckinghamshire and Oxon Naturalists Trust, *BBONT Nature Reserves,* BBONT

John Feltwell, (1995), *The Conservation of Butterflies in Britain, past and present,* Wildlife Matters

R. Gabb and D. Kitching, (1992), *Dragonflies and Damselflies of Cheshire,* National Museums and Galleries of Merseyside

B. Gibbons, (1986), *Dragonflies and Damselflies of Britain and Northern Europe,* Hamlyn

C.O. Hammond and R. Merrit, (1983), *The Dragonflies of Great Britain and Ireland,* Harley Books

N. Hammond, (1983), *RSPB Nature Reserves,* RSPB

Jeremy Hywel-Davies and Valerie Thom, (1986), *The Macmillan Guide to Britain's Nature Reserves,* Papermac

John Law, (1995), *Butterflies of Britain – a site guide,* Private

A. MacGeeney, (1986), *A Complete Guide to British Dragonflies,* Jonathan Cape

R. Merrit, (1996), *Atlas of the Dragonflies of Britain and Ireland,* HMSO

Norfolk Wildlife Trust, *The Norfolk Wildlife Trust Reserves Handbook,* Norfolk Wildlife Trust

Suffolk Wildlife Trust, *Suffolk Wildlife Trust Reserves Handbook,* Suffolk Wildlife Trust

J.A. Thomas, (1992), *Butterflies of the British Isles – Hamlyn Guide,* Hamlyn

J. Thomas and R. Lewington, (1991), *The Butterflies of Britain and Ireland,* Dorling Kindersley

INDEX TO BUTTERFLY SPECIES

Target species in the text, plus selected other species, are included in the index. Numbers refer to the sites.

INDEX TO DRAGONFLY SPECIES

Target species in the text, plus selected other species, are included in the index. Numbers refer to the sites.

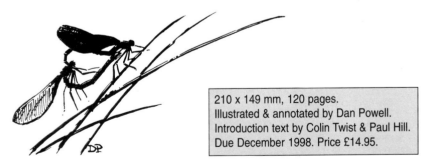